In recent years, through Kirlian photography and experiments with plants, scientists have postulated the theory of the L-field as the blueprint of life and a forcefield of energy which can be observed and photographed with either scientific instruments or this specialized photography which uses neither camera nor lens.

Suddenly now, after thousands of years of blindness and of the blind following the blind, mankind have awakened to new planes of Matter that exist and can be verified just beyond concrete Matter. What a vast area of exploration and discovery experiments in parapsychology have opened, and mankind are once again pushing back the frontiers of knowledge!

Hierarchy would provide extraordinary insight into the delvings of scientists, and especially those who are in fields of research that probe beyond the present bounds of finite existence.

Man is on the brink of discovering the Higher Self.

Djwal Kul

DJWAL KUL INTERMEDIATE STUDIES OF THE HUMAN AURA

Dictated to the Messenger
Elizabeth Clare Prophet

SUMMIT UNIVERSITY ❤ PRESS®

Intermediate Studies of the Human Aura
by Djwal Kul
Dictated to the Messenger Elizabeth Clare Prophet

Library of Congress Catalog Card Number: 75-19605
International Standard Book Number: 0-916766-13-6

This book is set in 11 point Baskerville with 1 point lead.
Printed in the United States of America
First Printing: 1976. Second Printing: 1977. Third Printing: 1980
Fourth Printing: 1981. Fifth Printing: 1983. Sixth Printing: 1985
Seventh Printing: 1987

Cover design: Drawing of *The Risen Christ* by Michelangelo.

SUMMIT UNIVERSITY ☙ PRESS®

Mark L. Prophet

Elizabeth Clare Prophet

Contents

4 *Contents*

To the Reader

The human body is a conductor of energy. The brain alone is composed of over ten billion nerve cells over which travel electrical impulses at speeds up to two hundred miles an hour. But energy flows in, through, and around the body in many forms — from measurable electrical impulses to higher forms of energy sometimes referred to as vital force, spiritual light, or prana.

One of the most recent and most astonishing discoveries relative to the energy fields that influence man has been that of the human aura. Although discussion of the aura is not unique to this age, the invention of the Kirlian camera has enabled scientists to photograph this forcefield that surrounds every man, woman, and child. Medical researchers at Harvard and Yale have concluded that the study of the aura can be an invaluable aid in the prevention of disease before it manifests in the physical form.

But science has yet to provide answers for many of the unsolved mysteries of the aura. Where does the aura originate? What effect or

control does it exert on the health of an individual? Does it influence human behavior? How
does the aura relate to our spiritual growth? Is
there any significance to the coloration of the
aura? And perhaps the most pertinent question of
all, Can we control or influence the human aura?

The answers to these questions are revealed
in the pages of this book. In *Intermediate Studies
of the Human Aura,* Djwal Kul provides valuable
instruction concerning the aura that will establish
precedent for decades to come. A sequel to
Studies of the Human Aura by Kuthumi, this
work was originally published as a series of letters
from Djwal Kul to his students throughout the
world. His discussion concerning the chakras
within the body as transmitters of light energy
is essential to the understanding of spiritual evolution. He gives numerous meditations and techniques for the clearing of the chakras and the
concentration of the "sacred fire" in the chakras
as the foundation for the expansion, the mastery,
and the projection of the aura in what he calls the
macrocosmic-microcosmic interchange.

In the words of Djwal Kul, "The purpose of
this intermediate series is to acquaint the student
with the specifics of the application of the law
and the light for the surrender of the lesser self,
for the sacrifice of all forms of self-indulgence,
and for the affirmation of true being here and
now in the very plane of awareness where you find
yourself a son or a daughter of God."

To Those Who Seek a Living Master

There comes a time in the life of the one who is seeking God when the soul reaches out for guidance on the Path. Only so long can he make it alone kicking against the pricks[1] of life and perhaps even against the very presence, albeit invisible, of the Lord God himself. By and by as life's disappointments—personal sorrow and personal failure—are experienced, the soul moved by true humility born of the pain of adversity kneels before the Lord and claims the Saviour as teacher, guide, and friend along the homeward way.

In East and West, the Saviour has been known in many chosen servants of the one God. In the West the Lord Christ incarnate as Jesus has been for millions not only the personal Saviour, but the living Master. Today there are many who count themselves disciples of Christ as that Christ was manifest in Jesus, in the perfect life he led and in the perfect law he taught. In the East those who would pursue the path of holiness (wholeness) have followed various masters, such as Gautama Buddha, Lord Maitreya, Confucius, Lao-tse, Bodhidharma, and Ramakrishna. Some follow teachers who are currently embodied; some follow those who have incarnated over the past centuries and are recognized to be in higher dimensions of being, or nirvana. But one and all have recognized that God, as he appears in every age through the living master, is indeed the instrument of salvation.

Many Christians have made the decision to confess, by the power of the Holy Spirit, that Jesus Christ is Lord. They have committed their lives to him. And in the day and the hour of their commitment, they know that their souls have truly been saved by the Lord. This relationship, which millions share with Jesus Christ, when understood, is altogether in keeping with the path of hierarchy and the initiations of the Great White Brotherhood. For the Great White Brotherhood is composed of a body of living masters—specifically, of those who have mastered time and space and ascended into the Presence of God, the I AM THAT I AM. [2]

Every one of these masters has fulfilled on earth the requirement of the attainment of the Christ consciousness which Jesus demonstrated in his life and work. As Jesus showed the path of initiation and of overcoming that leads to the individual transfiguration, the individual crucifixion, the individual resurrection, and the individual ascension, so many other sons and daughters of God on this and other worlds have also proved the laws of God which are applicable to and for all, seeing that He is no respecter of persons. [3]

In other epochs, in other worlds and systems of worlds, the incarnation of the Word has been a rhythmic fulfillment of the law of hierarchy. Responding to this law, souls have, through the ritual of renunciation, attached themselves to a living master, whether ascended, as in the case of Jesus, or unascended, as in the case of a select body of teachers chosen to represent the ascended hierarchy. Whether in the East or in the

West, the requirements and the relationship of the disciple to the Anointed One, of the chela to the guru, remain the same. In every case, the purpose of the relationship is to transfer the knowledge, the compassion, and the authority of the teacher to the disciple.

In those eras marked by the coming of an avatar, the flame of hierarchy, according to the laws of God, has been transferred on a one-to-one basis. For thousands of years the torch has been passed from teacher to disciple and then from the disciple who became the teacher to other disciples who in turn would pass it to succeeding generations. In church parlance, this transfer of light and grace and of the energies of the Holy Spirit is called apostolic succession. In the same way, priests and priestesses of the ancient temples of Lemuria and Atlantis passed on to neophytes in the temple the sacred art of intonation and invocation as God was worshiped in the flame of sacred fire burning on the altar.

In the past decade many seekers after God have recognized that the search for him can be fulfilled only through a living master. Many have sought that master in the gurus of the East. Still others have come before the Lord Jesus with renewed fervor and dedication. Both experiences are valid on the path of initiation leading to the attainment of self-mastery.

During the same period, the ascended masters — masters living in dimensions of cosmic consciousness to which they have attained through the initiation of the ascension — have come forth to call their disciples from among embodied mankind. These disciples were recognized by the masters because they themselves recognized just beyond the veil of time and space the individualized Presence of God in beings perfected, beings made whole through the fulfillment of the law of love. These chelas have sought their living master

among the gurus who have transcended the planes of
Matter and gone on to pave the way for life ascending
into the planes of Spirit.

The ascended masters are contacting mankind
today in a very real way. Through the power of the
spoken Word, they are reaching not only their chelas,
but all who will hear the true message of Jesus Christ,
of salvation, and of the individual Christ Self. For in
the ultimate sense the Christ Self is the real guru of
every man, woman, and child. The ascended masters
are touching people's lives in many ways — through love
and inspiration, through the sense of the helping
hand, the unseen yet uplifting presence, through the
spark of creativity and the elevation of mankind into a
greater and greater desire for peace with honor, for
integrity in government, and for the restoration of the
economies of the nations to the true law of the abundant life.

The ascended masters bring forth no new religion, nor are they engaged in polemics disputing doctrine and dogma in the various churches of the world.
Their teaching is designed to quicken hearts and
minds to that which is already understood in the
silence of the soul. Their teaching is for the awakening
of the soul to its inner potential, to the inner teacher,
the Christ Self of each one, and to the overshadowing
Presence of God, the I AM THAT I AM. The law that
is set forth is the law that is already written in the
inward parts of man.[4] The masters' purpose is to
awaken mankind to the fact that everyone does indeed
have a living master — first in his own Christ Self and
then in ascended ones, those who have realized the
potential of this Christ Self and returned to the plane
of Spirit, the octaves of perfection.

As you find your inner being affirming the truth
of the masters, there is developed a trust that is the
foundation of the guru-chela relationship. This trust

does not come in the reading of one book or in the
hearing of one lecture. It is gained over years of study
and of experimentation with the laws and exercises
that are given, of walking and talking with the
ascended masters, including Jesus and the Virgin
Mary, Gautama Buddha, John the Beloved, and many
of the saints who comprise the heavenly hosts.

Sometime you may find yourself reading a statement of the ascended masters that is in direct disagreement with your personal philosophy or your present awareness of life. When this happens, it is wise to
place your own beliefs, as well as the teaching of the
master, on the shelf, so to speak, and to wait for life
and new experiences to prove the rightness or wrongness of "my way" versus "their way." It is not necessary
to categorically accept or reject the teachings of the
ascended masters. What *is* necessary is that the seeker
prove step by step the truth of his own being and that
he never forsake the quest for living truth.

Just as many have come to the feet of Jesus and
have acknowledged him as their personal Saviour, just
as many have found in the East a teacher worthy of the
name, so you may come to the place where through the
study of the teachings of the ascended masters there is
sufficient trust and sufficient agreement for you to
place your hand in the hand of one of the ascended
hierarchy and say, "O living master, take my hand and
take me all the way home."

In that hour you will find yourself entering into
an intimate relationship with one of the ascended
masters — perhaps Saint Germain or El Morya,
Kuthumi or Maitreya. And you will find that with
each successive commitment to serve the master and
to assist him in his outreach for the enlightenment of
humanity, the master himself will come into your life
in a more personal way, giving personal counsel, personal discipline, and making plain the way of over-

coming through the daily surrendering of aspects of selfishness and self-centeredness to the attributes of selflessness and God-centeredness.

As you read and examine the writings of Djwal Kul, known to his chelas as the Tibetan Master, make an effort to enter into his consciousness. Then pray to God that he will send Djwal Kul to your side to guide and instruct you and to infuse your consciousness with his mastery, his vision, and his ever-gentle awareness of the eternal Presence. It is then your privilege to experiment with the teachings, with the path, and with the hierarchy. Unless you are willing to take part for awhile in the ascended masters' consciousness, you will never know whether or not their way can become your way.

The ascended masters are living masters. They are the teachers of the age. They are the teachers of all who are not content to accept life as it is being lived on this planet and who refuse to accept a defeatist attitude or a doomsday consciousness. The ascended masters are the teachers of those who are looking with hope to a new day, a new age, and to the victory of life over death, of truth over error, and of love over every form of hatred.

Hierarchy extends its hand to you. You have but to place your hand in the hand of your own Christ Self and the living masters to find the answers to life's most perplexing questions. These manuscripts of the master Djwal Kul are presented as an invitation to the path of the Great White Brotherhood. May you find therein not only the truth that will set you free, but also the living master you have been seeking.

Elizabeth Clare Prophet

Messenger for the Great White Brotherhood

Ashram of the World Mother
Los Angeles, California

I

A Pulsation of Life Becoming Life

Children of the One God:
I address myself to those of you who have pursued
the auric studies set forth by my colleague and friend
the Ascended Master Kuthumi. And to all who have
not had the privilege of reading his words and
following the cadences of his thought as the ever-
widening circle of the aura of this blessed Brother of
the Golden Robe encompasses the world in the love-
wisdom of his heart, may I recommend that you do so.
For our studies here will be laid upon the foundation
which Kuthumi has laid.

To those who have not known me or my work with
the hierarchy, which was registered concurrently with
that of Morya and Kuthumi upon many disciples of the
masters both in the East and the West during the last
century and a half, may I introduce myself as the
Tibetan Master and as one who has chosen to expand
the love fires of the heart to woo mankind to the center
of Christ awareness where the balance of the threefold
flame perceives and is perceived by the fullness of that
mind which was in Christ Jesus.[1]

The motto of the brothers who keep the flame

of life with me on behalf of earth's evolutions is summarized in the words of the writer of the Book of Proverbs "Keep thy heart with all diligence; for out of it are the issues of life."[2] Some of our disciples who have followed with us the long trek in pursuit of the star of his appearing, the great I AM Presence of the Bethlehem babe, will recall that it was I who accompanied the Masters El Morya and Kuthumi to the place where Jesus was born.[3]

We came to pay homage to the heart of God made manifest as the heart of the Son of God. We came to adore the light of the Christos. We came with the wise dominion of the masters of the Far East to form a circle of protection around mother and child and to impart to Joseph an aura of protection for the flight into Egypt.

We come again in this series on a similar mission. We come to pay homage to the Christ aborning in the heart of children of God everywhere. We come to expand the circle of protection. We come to teach mankind to keep the fires of the heart with all diligence and to conserve the crystal-flowing waters of life that issue forth from this luminous fount of love, wisdom, and power. We come to show forth a trinity of the mastery of the aura.

And so brother Kuthumi has nobly stated his case for the expansion of soul consciousness through the aura. He has shown how, by replacing the personality patterns and perversions with soul consciousness — which you call, and that rightly so, solar awareness — you can increase the forcefield of the aura and use it to intensify the light of God on earth and to make of the aura the wedding garment of the Lord.

The work of Kuthumi given forth as an exercise in the expansion of the soul and its faculties reaching out to contact the Spirit of God is intended to awaken mankind from the sleep of the ages to a new perception

of life, a perception of God, through the faculties of
the soul. It is a work which all devotees of the sacred
fire may use to diligently begin the process of the
personal cleansing that is so necessary to the realization
of the consciousness of God. As you meditate, then,
with beloved Kuthumi, recognize that he has a
momentum of auric light which he extends from his
forcefield to your own for the specific purpose of
bringing about the quickening and the cleansing of
your soul consciousness.

As we proceed in these studies to expand and
expound upon his work, we pursue the action of the
Christ consciousness that develops from the mastery of
soul awareness. We begin then with our meditation on
the heart as the seat of the authority of the Christ
mind, as the altar of the love fires of being. And we
intend, as it is our assignment from the Darjeeling
Council, to present to mankind the noble example, the
precepts of the law, and the action of the sacred fire
that will clearly mark the way of the expansion of the
aura through the mastery of the Christ consciousness,
not only in the heart but in all of the chakras of being.

And when we have concluded these studies and
the souls of our chelas have become prototypes of the
Christed One, then the Master El Morya will set forth
his course on Advanced Studies of the Human Aura
presently being given to certain initiates of the white
fire attending classes in their finer bodies at the etheric
Retreat of God's Will in Darjeeling, India. As my own
humble effort is toward the plane of the Christ, so that
of the Lord of the First Ray will be toward the
development of God consciousness, not only for the
Aquarian age but for all ages to come.

O you who would become and put on the garment
of God, you who would practice his presence, take
this our threefold offering of gold, frankincense, and
myrrh, and pledge yourself anew to the Covenant of

the Magi⁴ as we come again—Melchior, Caspar, and Balthazar⁵—to salute the birth of the Christ and to inaugurate a light that will surely envelop worlds within and worlds to come. For this is the age of the coming of the sons and daughters of God!

In the heart there is a pulsation of life becoming life that is the established rhythm of the cosmos reflected from the heart of God to the heart of the Great Central Sun, through the heart of the Elohim, thence to all lifewaves evolving in time and space. The heart is the focal point for the flow of life individualized as the I AM Presence, the Divine Monad of individuality, and the Christ Self that is the personification of the reality of being for every soul. The heart is the connecting point for all being, for all self-consciousness. Through the heart all mankind are one; and through the heart the Christ of the One, the only begotten Son of the Father-Mother God, becomes the Christ of all lifewaves unfolding God's life throughout the cosmos.

Through obedience to the first and great commandment of the Lord, "Thou shalt love the Lord thy God with all thy heart and with all thy soul and with all thy mind,"⁶ the heart of man is wed to the heart of God and the alchemy of a life lived on earth even as it is lived in heaven is begun. The act of loving produces the action of the cosmic flow; and it is the flow of energy from the heart of man to the heart of God that rejuvenates the being of man, that strengthens the citadel of consciousness, that expands the auric forcefield, and that ultimately magnetizes the soul of man to the Spirit of God in the ritual of the ascension in the light.

It was love as he lived and breathed the essence of the Holy Spirit which paved the way for mastery in the life of Jesus, a way which became a spiral of ascending currents of love over which the soul fulfilled its immortal destiny, being received in a cloud of love,[7] the forcefield of his very own I AM Presence.

Through the threefold flame within the heart, the threefold nature of God is realized in man and in woman. How clear is the word of the Lord throughout the ages! Two thousand years ago and throughout an eternity before and after, the law remains. To love God with all thy heart is to attain his Christ consciousness; to love God with all thy soul is to attain his soul consciousness; to love God with all thy mind is to attain his God consciousness.

And so we build upon the rock, and no other foundation can be laid than that which is laid in Christ Jesus.[8] Understand, then, that obedience to the laws of God as these have been set forth by the great prophets and teachers of all time in the sacred scriptures of the world will lead you to the place where you can move forward in the cycles of self-mastery that are even now unfolding as the signs of the Aquarian age.

And the second great commandment that is like unto the first, "Thou shalt love thy neighbour as thyself,"[9] is the means whereby you realize that the love which God has placed within your heart, your soul, and your mind is also in every part of life. And therefore to love God in the heart, the soul, and the mind of friend and foe alike is to come into unity—into the union of the Spirit Most Holy that pervades all consciousness and being, worlds without end.

When you can love the self as the threefold action of God's consciousness, you will have fulfilled the first and great commandment. And when you can love every part of life as this great God Self individualized, you will understand why Jesus said that on these two commandments hang all the law and the prophets. For the law is the Alpha spiral of Father, and the word of the prophets is the *mater*-ialization of the Mother flame through the power of the spoken Word that completes the Omega spiral of God Self-awareness and enables man and woman to return to the point of origin in the Divine Whole.

O children of the sun, children of the sun, let the fires of Helios and Vesta be released now through your heart! Do not hold back this great conflagration of the sacred fire burning within you as the desire of God to love and to love and to love. Do not hold back the floodtides of love! Let your consciousness, your heart, be washed by the waters of the word of love.

And now let the sacred fires from God's heart inscribe within the auricle and ventricle of the heart the name of God, I AM THAT I AM, [10] for the receiving and the giving of the flow of love. And now, ye who would be priests and priestesses of the sacred fire, this commandment is for you: "If ye will not hear and if ye will not lay it to heart to give glory unto my name, saith the Lord of hosts, I will even send a curse upon you and I will curse your blessings: yea, I have cursed them already, because ye do not lay it to heart." [11] In the words of Malachi is the key to the dominion of the heart and the heart's energies.

The consecration of life, and of the blood as the essence of life, with the name of God is like the consecration of the Eucharist. The consecration by the name of God is the process whereby the body and the blood of Jesus became the body and the blood of the Lord. When you participate in the ritual of Holy Communion, you assimilate that substance of the bread and the wine which have become, through transubstantiation, the body and the blood of the Christ. Now then, in our meditation upon the heart, you see how the altar of the heart, situated in the center of the tabernacle of being, becomes the place where God's substance and his energy, consecrated by the priest who is each one's own Christ Self, takes on and is imbued with the aura and the frequencies of the Holy Spirit.

Precious ones, we begin at the beginning. "If ye will not lay it to heart to give glory unto my name," no amount of study or endless pursuit of the chronicles and rituals of the chosen people will lead you to the awareness of the I AM THAT I AM. Jesus illustrated this law in this wise: "Whosoever shall deny me before men, him will I also deny before my Father which is in heaven." [12] The curse that returns upon those who turn away from the angel of the Lord who comes to impress the name of God, I AM THAT I AM, upon the heart is the curse of death and decay, disease and disintegration. This is the personal-impersonal action of the law of love which returns to mankind that which mankind have sent forth.

Understand and meditate upon this simple yet profound precept: Unless the energies of Mater be consecrated in all ways by the flame of the Spirit, their cycles will pass as the grass withereth and the flower fadeth. [13] From dust to dust [14] proceed the cycles of materialization until these are imbued with the cycles of Spirit. And when it comes to pass that man within his heart determines to give glory unto the name of the Lord, the being that is corruptible in Matter becomes incorruptible in Spirit and the cycles of Spirit and Matter merge in the expressions of the sons and daughters of God who walk the earth as Christed ones prepared to be received in the heart of God.

Won't you meditate upon this teaching in all humility as you offer the Introit to the Holy Christ Flame [15] in preparation for my next release on the heart.

Ever enfolding you in the trinity of love, I AM

Djwal Kul

II

The Name of God Is the Key

To Those Who Walk Not after the Flesh,
    but after the Spirit:
    Heart friends of the ages, I come to you in the
company of the hidden man of the heart,[1] your own
Christ Self. I come as a teacher; and yet I bow before
your own mentor of the Spirit, the mediator who
is Christ the Lord. For as I instruct the outer consciousness according to the precepts of the inner
law, it is the Christ, the light of the manifestation
which you call your self, who releases inspiration,
intuition, and intelligence from the seat of authority
that is the heart chakra. Concentric rings of illumination expand from the heart center as a golden-
pink glow ray, and the aura of man expands from
the center of the heart proportionately as levels of
awareness in the four lower bodies are purified to
become receptacles of God's light.
    Those who walk after the flesh[2] allow the concerns
of the flesh, the outer senses, and the world of material
things to fill the four lower bodies with the memory
of experiences, impressions, data, facts and figures
of all kinds. They allow emotions and sympathetic

attractions within the mass consciousness, not to mention the effluvia that collects in the physical body itself, to cave in on the heart chakra, to stifle the flow of energy through it, and to prevent the natural flow of the spiral of the Christos through the vehicles that are provided solely for the experience and the expansion of soul consciousness.

Those who walk after the Spirit are those who exert the will to press the light of the heart outward into manifestation in a spiral of glory for the fulfillment of the law of the Christ in the four lower bodies. Walking after the Spirit, these do not fear to replace the anxieties of the flesh that have taken hold in the four lower bodies with the verities of the eternal Spirit. To these, that which some have considered the pain of surrender or the so-called sacrifices of the spiritual path are neither painful nor sacrificial, but the entering-in to the joy of the Lord, the joy of communion in the flame and of congruency with the law.

Once you have accepted the gift of the angel who comes with the flaming sword to write upon the heart forevermore the name of God, I AM THAT I AM, this gift can never be taken from you, except it be by your own betrayal of that name and that flame. Like the law that is written in the inward parts of man,[3] in the core of every cell and atom of life, so the name of God written in the heart reverses the process of the law of sin and death and frees you for the law of the Spirit of life which was in Christ Jesus[4] and in every other Christed one who has walked the earth by the grace of God.

Thus the righteousness of the law is fulfilled in those who walk not after the flesh, but after the Spirit as the spiral that proceeds from the threefold flame within the heart, qualifying the energies of the physical, emotional, mental, and etheric bodies with

the frequencies of the Holy Spirit. Once the name of
God is written in the heart in fire, once the entire being
and consciousness of man moves daily, hourly to live
that law, to expand that fire, to glorify the name of
God, then the light of the heart fills the being and
consciousness of man until he becomes a blazing sun of
righteousness.

Now understand, then, the sacred writing "To be
carnally minded is death, but to be spiritually minded
is life and peace."[5] It is a question of alchemy; it is a
question of attention. The alchemy of your attention is
part of the gift of consciousness whereby through the
faculties of concentration—even the seven chakras of
the being of man—you focalize energy for a purpose.
Whether that purpose is life or death must forever be
the determination of your free will. Therefore, to be
carnally minded is death, but to be spiritually minded
is life and peace.

"Choose you this day whom ye will serve!"[6]
thunders the voice of God. And the initiate standing
before the mount of God-attainment must make the
decision whether to the right or to the left of the wye.
And the wye is you. Which you will you become? You
can be life or you can be death. You can fulfill the
spirals of life through the outward flow of the spirals of
the heart. You can fulfill the spirals of death by
allowing all that is carnal to destroy the last vestiges of
spirituality, until the flame within the heart is extin-
guished in the process that is known as the death of
the soul.

I call to your attention, O chelas of the sacred
fire, as we begin to impel the soul higher and higher in
the walk with God, that to take this teaching and to
employ it for the glorying in the Lord is to rise into the
dominion of the Spirit and to be, with Christ, alive
forevermore.[7] But to retain the intellect as the
perversion of God consciousness, to enthrone the ego in

place of the Christ, and to allow the human will and the human personality to replace the destiny of the soul and its individuality is to enter the negative spiral that cycles through the long night of carnality which terminates in self-annihilation.

The carnal mind is enmity against God because it is not subject to the law of God.[8] Because the carnal mind exalts the human ego in place of the Divine Ego, it is impossible for it to merge with the positive spirals of the Christ consciousness. Those who remain in the consciousness of the flesh, which consciousness is governed by the carnal mind, therefore cannot please God, because while they remain in that consciousness, they cannot conform with his laws. You who would come with me into a greater awareness of God, you who would have the gift of greater power, greater wisdom, and greater love, must understand that the filaments of mortal identity must be replaced with the filaments of immortal Selfhood.

In order for you to be successful in this course, then, I recommend that you go before the altar of God, before the threefold flame within, that you kneel before that altar within the tabernacle of your own heart and make your commitment to Almighty God to defend truth, honor, and righteousness in his name. You cannot remain neutral. For to fail to render a decision, to fail to make a choice, is in itself a decision. It is a choice, although a not-choice. To be the not-self is still recorded in the Book of Life as a choice.

Once you have made the commitment to defend the light as the energy of the Christ, to expand the flame of God and to glorify his name, you will stand forth as the sun in its zenith and you will know a power and a flow, an expansion of your aura, and an increase in the fires of the heart, the likes of which you have not seen in many incarnations. Therefore, in this release on the heart, I cannot fail to make known to you that the simple yet compelling act of unswerving devotion, of absolute conviction to be and to follow the Christ and to take both an active and a passive stand for Christ, is the sure way to transcend the former state of limitation and to live in the light of heaven and earth forevermore. Truly you have not begun to develop the aura, to expand the consciousness, until you have made this commitment and until the name of God is written in your heart.

Those who choose the left arm of the wye, to live for the carnal mind and the lusts of the flesh and the pride of the intellect, openly profess their amorality; and their code is the code of pleasure and their cult is the cult of death. They pay allegiance to Satan while denying his identity, not realizing that they are the dupes of the archdeceivers of mankind who pretend that death is life and that life is death. By thus distorting reality, they fool those who pride themselves in making fools of the children of God. Indeed, "there is a way that seemeth right unto a man, but the end thereof are the ways of death."[9]

And so the prophet Malachi foretold the judgment and the death of the wicked: "For, behold, the day cometh that shall burn as an oven; and all the proud, yea, and all that do wickedly shall be stubble: and the day that cometh shall burn them up, saith the Lord of hosts, that it shall leave them neither root nor branch."[10] This is the end of those who misuse the energies of the heart and the light of the Christ.

Before imparting unto you, then, the secrets of the heart, before unlocking the crystal fires of the heart in those who take their vow before the living God, I must make clear that since the day when God bestowed free will upon man and woman, there have been those who have gone to the right and there have been those who have gone to the left. And

the name of God is the key to their allegiance. For
unto those who fear the name "I AM THAT I AM"
shall the Sun of Righteousness arise with healing in
his wings! [11]

The rising of the Son of Righteousness is the rising
of the Christ consciousness. And it is the Christed ones
who shall tread down the wicked, and the spirals of the
wicked shall be as ashes under the soles of the feet of
the Christed ones until the prophecy is fulfilled "And I
will put enmity between thee and the Woman and
between thy seed and her seed; it shall bruise thy head,
and thou shalt bruise his heel." [12]

You live in the end of an age when the judgment
of God draweth nigh. All over the world, mankind are
making choices. Little do they know that the choices
they are making in little things and in great things will
soon be tallied, and they will be weighed in the
balances to see whether the majority of the soul is on
the side of the light and the law or on the side of
darkness and chaos.

To all who would continue in these *Intermediate
Studies of the Human Aura,* I say, beware! For if you
have failed to choose God and his Christ, it would be
well for you to refrain from entering the path that
leads to the holy of holies. For those who enter there
without the wedding garment that marks the surrender
of the soul to the Cosmic Virgin will be consumed by
the fires of God. [13]

Choose you this day whom ye will serve. And
having chosen aright, come with me as we proceed
to release, one by one, certain techniques for the
expansion, the control, and the empowering of the
aura essential for Christed man and Christed woman
to enter the golden age of Aquarius. I await the
sounding of your commitment upon the sounding
board of life. And when it is written in the book of
record by the recording angels, I will come to you and

make my presence known to you as the Tibetan Master
come again to deliver the word of God to the age.

I AM committed to your God-reality,

Djwal Kul

III

The Inner Geometry
of the Interlaced Triangles

My Beloved in Christ:
Let us enter into the consciousness of the heart.
"Draw nigh to me, and I will draw nigh to you"[1] are the
words of the Lord spoken within the soul of the Apostle
James as the key to the union of God and man through
the blessed mediator, the Christ Self. This union has
been depicted in the symbol of the six-pointed star —
the interlaced triangles that reveal the energies of man
ascending and the energies of God descending.

The point at which these energies meet is the
point within the heart chakra that is the threefold
flame of life. Let it be realized that the threefold flame
itself is the flaming consciousness of the Christ, the
only begotten of the Father, that is anchored within
every individualization of the Father-Mother God,
every son and daughter of the flame.

As you know, all energy has frequency, or vibra-
tory rate, but you must understand that the frequencies of man's energies are not the same as the
frequencies of God's energy. For the Lord God has
said, "My thoughts are not your thoughts; neither are
your ways my ways."[2] In order for God and man to be

one on earth even as the soul of man is one with the
Spirit of God in heaven, the Christ comes forth to
mediate the frequencies of Matter and of Spirit. The
perfect blending of the energies of God and man are
realized, then, through the Christ Self of the individual
or through masters ascended or unascended who have
attained the harmony of the Christ mind.

When Paul said, "Let this mind be in you which
was also in Christ Jesus," [3] he spoke of the Christ Self
and he directed the disciples of the Lord to let the
Christ Self be within their hearts the mediator of
perfection. The mind of which Paul spoke has been
referred to as the *higher mental body*. The terms
"higher mental body" and "Christ Self" are synon-
ymous, and they refer to the force or presence of
the Christos—even to the Logos who becomes the
Word incarnate to every son and daughter who
recognizes his joint heirship with the Christ. [4]

To fulfill then the first half of the equation "Draw
nigh to me, and I will draw nigh to you," mankind
must raise the energies of consciousness to the level of
the heart through meditation on love, through the
application of wisdom, and through the garnering of
God's energy as the will to be. As you center your
attention more and more upon the heart through the
visualizations, precious indeed, imparted to you by our
brother Lanello, [5] you magnetize the energies of the
four lower bodies day by day to the heart center, thus
according the Christ the preeminence and the dominion of your soul awareness.

The magnet that you create within the heart is the
ascending triangle. And the more you meditate upon
this triangle superimposed upon the heart, the more it
becomes the reality of the dimensions of the Sacred
Trinity in manifestation. As surely as the call compels
the answer, so the presence of this forcefield, of this triangle, combined with the letters of living flame "I AM

THAT I AM," will draw the descending triangle of God's consciousness into the heart. And this merging of Creator and creation through the intercession of the Christ Self and the Christ flame is the foundation of our exercise whereby the aura of man becomes the aura of God.

In God's holy name, O mankind, I say, awake from the sleep of the ages! In God's holy name, I say, do you not understand that you can become only that which you already are? If you would expand your aura as the forcefield of consciousness, you must possess the matrix within the heart for that expansion. The matrix is the six-pointed star centered over the threefold flame superimposed with the name of God, I AM THAT I AM. Now the second half of the equation is fulfilled as the Lord God himself declares, "I will draw nigh to you."

Down through the ages, many have said: "Why do I need Jesus or Buddha or Confucius or the Virgin Mary to get to God? I will go straight to God. I will bypass all others." And thus in their ignorance, mankind have displaced the Christed ones. Understand, then, that the law of intercession by the Christ is scientific and mathematical. It is based on the inner geometry of the interlaced triangles and on the science of the frequencies of material and spiritual energies.

In those periods of history when mankind have ignored the fact that the Christ light has ignited the flame within the heart as the gift of life and consciousness to *every* soul,[6] in the days when mankind see through a glass darkly and do not yet behold the Lord face to face as the Christ within themselves,[7] the Divine Presence has sent intermediaries — avatars, teachers, and prophets — who have exemplified the Christ light personified as the Christ Self of each and every one.

Until mankind come to know the Christ as the inner self, they may, according to cosmic law, appeal to the saints and holy ones both on earth and in heaven who, as Christed beings, intercede for them that they might merge their energies with the beloved I AM Presence. By and by, as the merging is reinforced by faith, by hope, by works of charity, one by one the children of God come to know the Christ Self within as their own individualized mediator, their own Christ consciousness. And as this truth is realized, their auras become the aura of God, and the halo of the saints, as the crown of glory, rests upon them as the grace of the Holy Spirit.

The aura of man marks the circumference of his awareness of God. It is a forcefield in Matter which God has created as an extension of himself—of his own God Self-awareness. The size of the aura is directly related to the individual's mastery of the frequencies of God's energies within the chakras—the key chakras being the seven most commonly referred to by Buddhists and Hindus as the wheels of life and death.[8] As the Christ becomes the light of the world of each chakra, so the energies of God and man meet in that chakra; and in this alchemical union—the balance of the triangles of Alpha and Omega and the converging of the energies of God and man—there is precipitated the law of perfection as the flame of living truth.

The aura of man is like a giant balloon; and this balloon is filled with neither oxygen nor helium, but with the flow of energy that is released from the seven chakras. The greater the energy that is released, the greater the size of the balloon. The greater the size of the balloon, the more God can release his consciousness into the planes of Mater. For the balloon is the coordinate in time and space of the great causal body of the Father-Mother God.

Each of the chakras has a special function, and we shall consider these functions step by step. Each of the wheellike vortices that comprise the chakras has, according to the teachings of the masters of the Himalayas, a certain frequency that is marked by a number of petals, so-called. These petals determine the flow of the energies of God to man, and they govern certain aspects of God's consciousness, commonly called virtues, which may be amplified within the chakras.

The chakras that are presently operative in the being of man are anchored in the *lower etheric body,* and their positions conform to the organs in the physical body which receive the flow of vitality from the higher bodies necessary to its functioning. These chakras are located at the base of the spine, over the spleen, over the navel, over the heart, at the throat, on the brow, and at the crown. The placement of these chakras to correspond with nerve centers in the physical body was adjusted during the epoch of the Fall of Man. There remains, however, in the *higher etheric body* the line of the seven chakras as forcefields for the seven rays; and these are for the distribution in the four lower bodies of the frequencies of the seven Elohim, known as the seven Spirits of God.

At this point in our dissertation, we are concerned with the interaction and the flow of the energies of the heart chakra as these are divided into the twelve petals, frequencies or aspects, of the Christ consciousness. In order for mankind to attain the Christ consciousness, it is necessary for them to balance the threefold flame within the heart so that the threefold flame might be realized by the power of the four (four times three equals twelve) — marking the four sides of the temple of being. Students of cosmic law therefore pursue the externalization of the twelve sacred virtues in order to attain the mastery of the heart chakra; for they know that the heart as the seat of Christ-authority is the key to mastery in all planes — in all chakras.

This week as you meditate upon the fires of the

heart, I ask you to chant the name of God, I AM
THAT I AM, and then to call in the name of the
Christ for the following God-qualities to be focused
in the geometry of the twelve according to the distribution of frequencies in this lotus of twelve petals:
God-power, God-love, and God-mastery; God-control,
God-obedience, and God-wisdom; God-harmony, God-
gratitude, and God-justice; God-reality, God-vision,
and God-victory. You may also alternate your chant
of the sacred name with the AUM, or OM. These
chants, combined with the fervent application to your
God Presence to focus these frequencies within the
heart, will bring balance to both your inner and your
outer being and restore the equilibrium of the Christ
flame that is so often lost in the wild and the welter
that marks your "modern" civilization.

> So now, my beloved in Christ,
> My gift of love, a cup of light,
> A cup of illumination rare,
> I bring to you as holy prayer.
> It is *my* prayer that you become
> The fullness of his glory.
> It is *God's* prayer
> That his energy we share.
> So, my beloved,
> Let it be *your* prayer
> That Almighty God will be there
> As virtue flowing, as light all-knowing
> In the center and the circumference
> Of the sacred center,
> Sacred fire of the heart.

I AM in the Buddha the turning of the wheel of
the law,

Djwal Kul

IV

The Challenge of the Carnal Mind

To Those Who Would Be Just Stewards
  of the Law and the Flame:
  If you are in earnest in your determination to
expand the aura, it is time that you challenge the
carnal mind even as Jesus challenged the Pharisees
who derided the Christ, saying: "Ye are they which
justify yourselves before men; but God knoweth your
hearts: for that which is highly esteemed among men is
abomination in the sight of God."[1] The carnal mind
deviously employs the human intellect, the human
emotions, and the human will to justify itself before
mankind; and thereby it gains the esteem of the world.
And thereby there is formed the personality that is
popular with the people.
  The carnal mind is the manipulator of the mass
energies of the mass consciousness. Since the carnal
mind is in control of the world, the flesh, and the devil,
Jesus said to the children of light, "Make to yourselves
friends of the mammon of unrighteousness; that, when
ye fail, they may receive you into everlasting habita-
tions."[2] Thus the Lord showed the initiates of the
sacred fire that there was a time to challenge the

carnal mind and a time to be wise in the ways of the world.

I come to distinguish these precepts of the law of the Father and of the grace of the Son, that you might understand your place in society. For the fire which you bear is not of this world, yet the frame that you wear is of the "earth, earthy." [3] When to agree with the adversary and when to disagree with the adversary, then, is a matter that must be settled once and for all. For to antagonize the carnal mind is most dangerous to our cause; to poke the sleeping serpent with a stick is to invite trouble.

You must understand that in many among mankind, the innocence of the soul predominates over the pride and the ambition of the ego; for in many, the ego has not been awakened as a deleterious force. The carnal mind has not been aroused, and therefore it has not overtaken the Christ Child cradled within the heart. These are the sheep of the Good Shepherd that are grazing upon the hillsides of the world waiting for the voice of the Son of God. Meek and mild are they, and without guile. They do not respond to the temptations of the tempter; for they are moved and impelled by the energies of the Holy Spirit, the momentum of the soul to move Godward.

Although their consciousness of God and Christ is the simple message of salvation in the Lord, yet they remain firm in their conviction of the promised one. The level of their awareness does not compel the search for the understanding of the complexities of the law. We do not challenge their belief. We remand their souls to the cloudlike forcefields of the Holy Spirit, which seal them in the love of God until that age when they shall find themselves in another fold of the Creator's consciousness, prepared to receive the strong meat of the Word. [4]

Take care, O chelas of the masters, as you walk

among the flocks of the Good Shepherd, that you do
not arouse the carnal mind that remains dormant in
these blessed ones — whether by direct confrontation,
by challenging their seemingly simplistic view of life,
or by superimposing upon their hearts and minds grids
and forcefields of God's consciousness that will
prematurely rend the veils of innocence, causing them
much grief, unnecessary guilt, and even despondency.
With these, the precepts and the parables of the Christ
will form a common meeting ground of heavenly love
abiding on earth, sealing the bonds of brotherhood
and allowing for the free expression of the faith of the
Galilean Master. For freedom of religion is a tenet of
the law and of the Lord that allows for agreement in
disagreement, whereby the children of God agree to
disagree in love, in respect, and in honor for the many
rays of the Son consciousness that lead to the one path
of the ineffable light.

To impose the teachings of the ascended masters
upon those who are unprepared to receive them
because the Christ is yet a babe and the carnal mind
doth sleep can truly be an imposition whereby carnal
energies are stirred and the child is overpowered by the
strong meat when the milk of the Word would suffice.
Take care, then, that you do not preempt the cycles of
the Creator when dealing with the sheep of the many
folds of God's heart. And realize that an encounter
with anyone is always an exercise in the psychology of
the Christ as well as in the psychology of the carnal
mind. It is always an opportunity to balance these two
factors of identity so as to produce the greatest soul
advancement and the greatest blessing to all.

When you encounter those such as the covetous
Pharisees, the hypocrites, and the children of this
world, you find that the carnal mind is not only
awakened, but that it has total command of the
consciousness. And it is absolutely necessary to deal

with that mind and its energies at its own level. In this instance, it is mandatory that in the devotee the fire of the heart remain sealed in an ovoid, and that in all relationships with the earth-minded, the devotee allow that aspect of himself which equates with the form and the form consciousness of the "earth, earthy" to predominate. Thus the carnal-minded may entertain the spirits of the flaming ones without reacting or overreacting to the light that is encased within the form, and thus you can make your way in this world and make a mark for the Lord free of the encumbrances of the carnal mind.

It is not necessary to make those whose consciousness is dominated by the carnal mind uncomfortable in your presence by spouting platitudes and displaying holy virtue or condemning amorality. This is but to arouse the antagonism of the world; and to put it bluntly, it is no way to win friends and influence people for the light. When there are so many souls receptive to the teaching and the inner fires of the heart, why bring upon the masters, our emissaries, and our organization a holocaust of controversy from those who are already committed to the way of the lesser self?

And so to agree with thine adversary quickly while thou art in the way with him [5] can also be a means of learning the mastery of time and space in the cycles of Mater. And you may learn the lesson of faithfulness in the responsibilities of the world whereby, working among the mammon of unrighteousness which is built in to the very structure of civilization itself, you may by and by learn the mastery of the coils of the Spirit and therefore have committed to your trust the true riches because you have been faithful in the "unrighteous mammon."

There comes a time in the life of every disciple when the injunction "Resist the devil, and he will flee from you!" [6] must be obeyed. In that moment there is no substitute for the fierce rebuke of the Christ "Get thee behind me, Satan!"[7] While the evolving soul consciousness is to be forgiven seventy times seven,[8] the serpentine mind that would override the innocence of the soul must be firmly put in its place and kept there. Above all, take care that you do not destroy "these little ones"[9] while you are destroying the carnal mind.

Now then, if you are still perplexed concerning what may seem to be a double standard of the presentation of the law and the promulgation of the prophecies of the prophets, I will let you ponder my words and juggle for a bit the ball-like precepts, variegated in hue, with which the fingers of the mind must become familiar if you are to advance in the higher studies of the human aura. For you see, as you rise in the dimensions of the Christ consciousness, you will begin to realize that every teaching of the law and every parable of the Christ gains new meaning as you approach closer and closer to the center of the heart.

Let us take, then, as an example of this spiritual phenomenon the statement of the Lord "The law and the prophets were until John [meaning John the Baptist]; since that time the kingdom of God is preached, and every man presseth into it."[10] Do you see that this is exactly what I am talking about? In a certain dimension of consciousness for a cycle of two thousand years, the law and the prophets as these are expressed in the Old Testament predominated as the rod of understanding—the lexicon of learning. But with the coming of John the Baptist, who prepared the way for the Christ, suddenly the kingdom of God— "behold, the kingdom of God is within you"[11]—is preached, and every man, not the privileged few, presses into this kingdom that is within.

I would also speak of the kingdom of God that is within you in reference to the heart chakra. For the kingdom of God that must come into manifestation in the planes of Mater begins with the flame within the heart, the petals or frequencies of God's consciousness externalized there, the six-pointed star, the I AM THAT I AM. But particularly the kingdom begins with the hidden chamber of the heart. I would speak of this chamber as the house of the Lord of which David spoke when he said, "Surely goodness and mercy shall follow me all the days of my life: and I will dwell in the house of the Lord for ever."[12] David knew his Lord as the hidden man of the heart dwelling in the hidden chamber of the heart. When David said, "The Lord is my shepherd; I shall not want,"[13] he spoke of his guru, his own Christ Self, upon whose law he meditated day and night.

Throughout all time, the sons and daughters of God who have come into the initiations of hierarchy have been received in sacred audience in the hidden chamber of the heart by the hidden man of the heart. To Hindus and Buddhists, this hidden chamber is the secondary heart chakra, an eight-petaled lotus which is identified just beneath the twelve-petaled heart chakra. It is the place where the chela contacts the guru. It is the place where the laws of cosmos are written in the inward parts of man. For the law is inscribed as the eightfold path of the Buddha upon the inner walls of the chamber.

Here the psalmist delighted in the law of the Lord.[14] Here he visualized, like his counterpart in the East, the sea of nectar, the island of gems, fragrant flowers, trees symbolizing the branches of spiritual teaching bearing the fruit of the Spirit. Here the Eastern devotee visualizes the platform and the throne constructed of fiery jewels. Here on the throne ensconced in lotus flame is the guru, the Christ Self, who receives the soul of the initiate. Here the psalmist also walked. Here he became like the tree of life planted by the rivers of water bringing forth the fruit, the flow of the energies of the heart chakra, in season and in cycle.[15]

This chamber is the sanctuary of meditation, the place to which the souls of the light-bearers withdraw. And here in this chamber we shall pursue the Master Presence, that each disciple of the Christ might come to know him as he is.[16] Thus God knoweth your hearts. And the pure in heart see God[17] within the chamber of the heart, whereas those who dwell in outer darkness, esteemed among men, are an abomination in his sight.

We shall continue our discourse to those who would become just stewards of the heart.

I AM your initiator in the flame,

Djwal Kul

V

The Hidden Chamber of the Heart

To Those Who Would Become Just Stewards
         of the Heart:
    To enter into the garden of the heart is to enter a
chamber that exists in the mind of God which can
come into being as the kingdom of God within you
through meditation and through visualization. The
Psalms were written as praises to the Lord whom David
knew as he entered this chamber. And so I bid you
enter also.
    This chamber is the place where the planes of
Mater are consecrated by the fires of the heart to the
very point of perfection. Thus the Eastern devotee
sees the earth transformed into jewellike crystals.
Emeralds, diamonds, rubies compose the island in the
midst of the nectar sea; and the essence of the Spirit
Most Holy is the fragrance from flowering trees. You
should also use your imagination to create this royal
scene befitting your own Christ Self and your
ascended-master guru.
    That you might attain the Christ consciousness of
the seven rays, I give to you the exercise of visualizing
each of the seven chohans (lords) of the rays. And thus

we will proceed step by step to expand the aura according to the masterful consciousness of these ascended-master gurus. The eight petals of the secondary heart chamber symbolize the mastery of the seven rays through the flame of the Christ (called the threefold flame) and the integration of that mastery in the eighth ray.

In all precipitation it is well to be specific. Therefore, draw a specific outline in your mind of this bejeweled island suspended in a glistening sea. Then see yourself walking from the shores of the sea through the tropical trees and vegetation to the center and highest promontory of the island. Tropical birds and flowers of delicate and brilliant colors make the scene more vivid. And by and by you hear the songs of the birds as they sing the song celestial and key the soul to the frequencies of that plane where the ascending triangle of Mater meets the descending triangle of Spirit.

When you come to the center of your island in the sun, visualize specifically the platform and the throne that are consecrated for the image and the sacred presence of the master. You may wish to examine historical works showing the most beautiful thrones that have been built for the kings and queens of this world. Select a design that is richly carved, gold leafed, and inlaid with precious and semiprecious stones, and visualize upon it a velvet cushion. There will be a cushion for each of the colors of the seven rays upon which the chohans will sit on the seven days of the week and receive you in the name of the Christ.

As you contemplate the blue-skyey dome and this place prepared to receive the Lord, give the following invocation for the integration of your soul with the consciousness of the Christ and its perfect outpicturing in the hidden chamber of the heart:

Almighty God, Maker of heaven and earth,
How bountiful are thy blessings!
How beautiful are thy flowings,
Immortal soul-knowings!
I acknowledge thee,
O thou Creator of me!
I acknowledge thy law
And the stars in the firmament
As the presence of the Christ
Who inhabits the cosmos,
As the boundaries of thy habitation
Here in the planes of *Mater*ialization
That reach like the rising and the falling
Of the waves of the sea calling
For the planes of the Spirit,
The reaches of infinity.

O Lord my God,
Come and talk and walk with me
In this my paradise garden,
My island in the sea!
Come, O Lord, in the cool of the day.
Come! For I have prepared the way,
And my offering is the sacrifice of the lesser self
Upon the altar of the heart.
My offering is the twelve virtues —
Oh, let the Christ now impart!
I kneel before the altar,
I kneel before thy throne.
My soul does long for unity,
The wisdom to atone.

O come, thou Divine Master,
The chohan of my life!
Come, O Lord,
In the form of El Morya,
Of Paul the Venetian and of Lanto.
Come, O Lord of heaven,

To consecrate my earth and my heaven.
Come with the truth,
With the freedom,
With the potential and the leaven.
Come, Serapis Bey, Hilarion!
Come, Nada and Saint Germain!
For I am not alone in the garden,
But all one with thee in thy name.
I AM THAT I AM, I AM THAT I AM,
    I AM THAT I AM—
Threefold action of threefold flame of threefold law.
So the name of God
Releases now the holy awe.

I come before thy presence, Lord.
I see thee in thy essence, Lord.
I am thy omnipresence, Lord.
O holy one of God,
Come now be the Christ of me
As the fulfilling of the law
Of the Personal Personality.
For in that flame and by thy name,
Ascended-master gurus do proclaim
That in the person of the Son of God,
The Christ, the Christed Self of all,
Becomes the mentor and the guide
And ultimately the flame
Of purest son and daughter pressed inside
The hidden chamber of the heart.

Teach me, O chohan of my life,
How to be thyself,
How to walk the earth
As heart and head and hand
Responding to thy will at thy command.
Teach me, O chohan of my love,
How to feel the flow,
How to give thy succor

>To all hearts below.
>Teach me now, O chohan of the law,
>To fulfill the promise of the seven rays
>And to be forevermore
>Prism'd awareness of thy grace.

O just stewards of the heart, understand how your aura can be enflamed with the presence of your Lord. And give this meditation as you renew your visualization of the chohans of the seven rays on the days of the week consecrated to those rays [1] by the impartations of Helios and Vesta, Father-Mother Presence of Life in the heart of this solar system where you make your home. Thus on Monday receive blessed Paul the Venetian and be tutored in the intuition and the mandates of love as he imparts creative fires and creativity of soul desire seated in the throne of the heart.

On Tuesday let your Christ Self lead you to the altar where you kneel before Lord Morya El, where you commune in silent meditation with the will of the flame and imbibe the Personal Personality of the one who has consecrated his mind as the diamond shining mind of God. And as you look upon his face, you see the twinkle of mirth that is needed upon earth. You hear the strains of "Panis Angelicus," and you know that your soul is fed the holy bread of angels. You drink the communion cup, and you vow obedience to the will of God.

On Wednesday as you contemplate the action of the emerald ray with joy and anticipation, you await the coming of Hilarion, who occupies the throne as the master philosopher, the master scientist. And from his forehead to your own, as the two of you are alone in Christ, there is a transfer of the divine gnosis; and the geometry of Mater integrating spirals of Spirit becomes clear.

On Thursday, the queen of the chohans, the Lady
Master Nada, who practices law before the bar of
heaven, comes to portray the law of justice and the
noble way of ministration and service. In her aura is
the music of those blessed words "Inasmuch as ye have
done it unto one of the least of these my brethren, ye
have done it unto me."[2] And in the presence of the lady
chohan, you perceive the wonder of the feminine ray in
the mastery of the seven rays. All is clear: You live to
serve forevermore — forevermore in the service of the
Lord.

On Friday you hail Serapis Bey, Lord of Ascension's Flame. Marching to the sound of victory, of
trumpets sounding the sound of your natal day, of
the soul's rebirth — being born anew first in Mater and
then in the glorious array of the ascension flame — you
are born into Spirit for eternity.

On Saturday that is the sabbath of the seventh
ray, you greet the Master of the Aquarian age: "Saint
Germain, friend of old, I am honored at thy presence
here! So may I know the cosmic honor flame that is
entwined with strands of gold and violet as elementals
weave a garland of praise to the Knight Commander of
my heart." And you tarry before the alchemist of the
Spirit who has come to teach you the science of the
amethyst ray and the ritual of grace that will be the
law for the next two thousand years.

On Sunday you rise to greet the dawn of
illumination through Lord Lanto, who holds in his
hands the book of the law of life for your soul — for the
soul of a planet and a universe. His wisdom is a scroll
that never ends; 'tis a scroll whereby you make
amends. And in the profound understanding of the
Lord of the Second Ray, lo, your sins are washed away!

Through the week with the seven chohans of the
rays is a way of life for Brothers of the Golden Robe,
for Sisters of the Wisdom Flame, who come to receive

the instruction that is given in the etheric retreat of the Tibetan Master. For many centuries now, I have sponsored the tutoring of souls who have desired to enter in to a direct relationship with one or more masters of the hierarchy of the Great White Brotherhood.

We begin our course with meditations for self-purification. And for those who have for several lifetimes practiced the way of silence, I come to break the silence with a shout of acclamation, with that joyful noise that is the true fiat of the Word! And thus the decrees of the devotees ring forth not as a murmuring or as a mumbling, but with the determined shout of warriors bold, of sons and daughters of God rejoicing in the fold![3] And the fold is a new level of awareness where the chela meets the master face to face and the energies of meditation become the fullness of the expression of the Christ mind, the Christ heart, and the Christ soul.

You who would become the Christ, you who would kneel at his feet, be prepared then to roar as lions over the hillsides of the world—not as the devil seeking whom he may devour,[4] but as king and queen, as lion and lioness going forth to claim dominion in the kingdom of God that is within. If you would attain and retain the consciousness of the chohans, you must then be willing to exercise the throat chakra whereby you take the energies garnered in the chamber of the heart, the fruits of the Spirit and the fragrance of the Spirit, and allow these gifts of the chohans to mesh in Mater through the peaceful thrust and the all-commanding power of the fiats of the Word.

Speak boldly, plainly—slow or swiftly as you will. Speak in rhythm. Speak in love. Speak in fervor and with zeal. But come before the presence of the chohans prepared to voice the soundless sound and to direct atoms and molecules of being by the authority and the grace of the law. Hence, as you develop the heart chakra and become a just steward of the heart, you must learn to release the resources of the Spirit through the spoken Word and to give decrees in time and space that are for the transmutation of that place into the dominion and the domain of the kingdom of God.

I am leading you gently yet firmly by the hand to that Promised Land where ascended masters yet walk and talk with unascended man. Come with me! Hold my hand!

Djwal Kul

VI

The Spectrum of God's Consciousness

To Those Who by the Flame of Obedience
  Would Earn the Flame of Wisdom's Love:
    As you advance in the knowledge of the law and
make progress on the path of self-mastery, you come
into the awareness of the love of the Father-Mother
God that is fulfilled in the law which is proclaimed by
the Son. To love the law of God is to be aflame with the
awareness of that law as it moves from the Impersonal
Impersonality of the Godhead to identification with
the Impersonal Personality of the sons and daughters
of God. For these, while retaining the impersonal
aspects of the Creator, do modify, by the flame of the
Christ, those energies of the law which become in
Matter as in Spirit the manifest personality of the
Divine One.
    And so we acknowledge the preceptors of man-
kind as beings who remain impersonal by the very
fact of the remoteness of the Spirit to the things of this
world. Yet they come forth as divine personalities,
ascended-master teachers, as the shining ones who
personify some facet of the jeweled splendor of his will,
his mind, and his compassion. Those who seek

to depersonalize all aspects of being, who count themselves sophisticated in their rejection of the "personality" of our messengers, both ascended and unascended, must realize that God is both the formed and the unformed. He is the Spirit that cannot be contained in form and yet who dwells immortally in form as the intelligent, free-flowing, sacred knowing of the fire that burns upon the altar of the heart of every son and daughter of God.

I speak to you who take pride in refraining from idolatry and the "superstitions" of the idolatrous generation: Take care that in your categorical rejection of the personality of God in the saints and ascended beings of all ages, you do not raise up in its place the human personality of the lower self. How often the intelligentsia, so-called, counting themselves to be above such childishness, have rejected the sacredness of the personality of God as it manifests above in the heavenly hosts and below in devotees, pilgrims, and disciples the world around. The elite who follow the cult of the serpent are the ones who worship the Moloch of human greed. Operating as they do outside the body of God, they are the electrodes of a mass entity that makes up the pseudo-personality of the Antichrist.

As you seek to master the science of expanding the forcefield of self-awareness which we call the human aura and which by practice can become the divine aura, let us set at naught the arguments of the ages concerning whether God as a Spirit is personal or impersonal.

Again it is a question of frequencies, a question of levels of identification. Man identifies with God through the centers called the chakras. Depending on where his consciousness is at the moment, he may see God as the Impersonal Impersonality—as the flaming Presence of the I AM THAT I AM, the Father

Principle, the Supreme Lawgiver—or he may identify with the Impersonal Personality of the Logos that is the Word made flesh,[1] the Christ incarnate in sons and daughters of the One who embody aspects of the seven rays of the Only Begotten of God.

On the other hand, he may become enamored with the most Personal Personality of the Godhead which bespeaks the Mother image and the Mother flame, the dearest and most tender, the gentlest and most flowing aspect of God. Then too, he may see God as the Holy Spirit, as cloven tongues of fiery Love[2] piercing the night and balancing the day star[3] right within the very heart and soul of man as the most Personal Impersonality of the Comforter.

Over the centuries of mankind's Godward evolution, the followers of various religions have centered on one or more of these levels of identification with God. The Impersonal Impersonality of the God of Israel was seen in the religion of the patriarchs, the commandments of the law, and the descent of the kings and prophets as father figures to both the Arabs and the Jews. The religion of the Christ centered in the concept of the incarnation of the Word as John the Baptist and Jesus illustrated by their example and their ultimate sacrifice the true nature of the Impersonal Personality of the Logos.

Whereas the religion of the Mother has appeared in and as the greatest cultures the world has ever known—for her flame precipitates science and invention, art and music, philosophy and mathematics—devotees of the World Mother address her according to the traditions of their lands—as Mary or one of the many feminine saints, as Kali or Durga, Vesta or Venus, Isis or Athena. Finally, those who have attuned to the delicate Presence that moves in the rushing mighty wind of the Holy Spirit[4] are those who in all ages have known no other religion but love—love as action, love as contemplation, love as the consuming fire,[5] love as "I AM my brother's keeper."[6] These are the mystics and the priests of the sacred fire, Zoroastrians and the spiritual lineage of Melchizedek,[7] members of holy orders and communities of the Spirit. Theirs is the practical realization of the most Personal Impersonality of the Godhead.

There are many paths, but all lead to the one Source of life. All are necessary to the balanced manifestation of God in man; and seeing that mankind in their state of limitation could not resolve the four aspects into one, the Lord God did create these religions to satisfy the diversity of temperaments that make up the many faces of humanity. And from East to West, the body of God on earth has realized the spectrum of God's consciousness, facet by facet, nation by nation. And who can say, observing the whole, who is right and who is wrong? It is not a question of rightness or wrongness, but one of wholeness and of the measure of a man.

These archetypes of God show forth at once his universality and his ever-present personality. Therefore, to know him as he is, mankind must realize that the four lower bodies are given for the realization of the God of very gods [8] who allows a portion of the Infinite Self to be seen, to be heard, and even to be recognized — yes, dear ones, in finite form. Not that we aver that man could ever contain the allness of God; but then, cannot God contain within himself the allness of man? And as man is contained therein, so can he not now become a portion of the Infinite Self? To deny this truth is to limit the ability of God to express himself in his most cherished creation — male and female made after the Self Image of the Divine Us.[9] And therefore it is written that one day the soul that has overcome will merge with the Presence of the I AM to realize the allness of that Self.

And so then, as you begin to press the aura of God
upon the aura of the world by your determination to
be holy vessels of that Holy Spirit, know that that
Spirit, through you, in you, can influence all of life. By
defining the lines of force as these compel Spirit's
energies to flow in Mater, you can deliver to the age
the mandate of God's awareness of himself as the
omnipotent Father-Mother, as the omniscient Logos,
and as the omnipresent Spirit.

Have you had success in your meditation with the
chohans of the rays? Have you entered into oneness
with the Christ Self through the communion of the
heart? Have those majestic impersonal personalities of
ascended Christed ones endeared you to the very
Person of God himself? Dare you think of such a
concept of the Person of God? Dare you think of
meeting that Person, whether here on earth or in the
flaming yod, sun center that all one day shall enter?

Do you understand that it is the nature of
Antichrist, of that force which opposes the pure
personalities of Christed ones, to deny the reality, yea
the necessity of the personification of the God flame?
And thus the Antichrist has convinced the worldly-wise
of the nonexistence of both the personality of God and
the personality of the devil. And thereby Antichrist
continues in many quarters unchallenged in his work
of tearing down the personality of Good while
reinforcing the personality of evil, all the while placing
upon it the mask of anonymity.

In a world where the lines of definition that mark
the individuality of those who strive for the goal of
perfection through the individualization of the Christ
flame of the seven rays grow less and less, it is essential
to proclaim the personality of the Christ as the
identifying mark of all who are born of the Father-
Mother God. In a world where the mass consciousness
is leveling mankind to a common denominator of the

human personality, where the herd instinct and animal passions govern the monotonous manifestations of egos who are becoming automatons—whether to a totalitarian state, a godless economy, a religion of rote formulae, or a runaway science—in a world where the definition of man and woman made in the image and likeness of God is becoming blurred as though seen through the mists of maya, it is imperative that all who are alert and awake as watchmen on the wall of life challenge the Antichrist. This should be done daily with the following fiat: "In the name of Jesus the Christ, I challenge the carnal mind, the Antichrist, and all satanic power in every man, woman, and child upon this planet!"

David gave the formula for beholding the Christ and holding the immaculate concept on behalf of the sons and daughters of God when he said, "Mark the perfect man, and behold the upright: for the end of that man is peace."[10] The identifying mark of all who are born of God is the point of light, of sacred fire, that expands from the heart through the rings of self-awareness which comprise the aura. This point of light pulsates in the forcefield of the aura as a unique identity recognizable to God and man both in heaven and on earth. Those who seek to deny this personality or to circumvent it as they steal the energies of the Spirit in the sin against the Holy Ghost[11] have the mark of the beast.[12] These are the idolaters in every age who reject the Christ, replace it with the lesser self, and proclaim that self as God.

We have initiated the cycle of your meditation with the chohans in order that you might put on and become the personality of the Christ as it is realized through the seven rays. And thus it is the work of each of the seven chohans to show you what your options are as you amplify the seven rays through the seven days of the week. These options are to be the most exact and exacting replica of the flame as Father, Mother, Son, and Holy Spirit define the personality of the Christ in each devotee of the light. By practicing this exercise, then, you will come to know the likeness of the Christ as it ought to manifest in your life in small ways and in big ways, in minutest detail and on a larger scale, as you expand here below the very specifications of the length and breadth and height and depth of the City Foursquare,[13] which is composed of the four elements (planes) of God's being within your body temples fair.

And thus while the heathen rage and the people imagine a vain thing,[14] while the dragon sends forth the flood to devour the Manchild who is the personality of God that is realized through the Woman,[15] while forces and forcefields and interplanetary rays are being sent forth from the evil one to erase, if it were possible, the very energies of the elect,[16] I stand forth with the teaching that will enable you to exert the power of the very living Presence of God as that Presence in you becomes personal wisdom and personal love individualized for all.

The communications of the chohans given to your soul upon the island suspended in the glistening sea are specifically for the individual needs of devotees on the Path. Therefore I say, raise up your voice! Raise up your energies of the heart to the level of the sixteen-petaled chakra of the spoken Word! And let the mastery of that chakra be in the communication of the ideations of God that have become the formulae of the Logos. Let the silence be broken as atoms and molecules coalesce through the fiats of the light to form within your own temple foursquare the sacred squaring of the hallowed Trinity!

You see, precious ones, the twelve petals of the heart that were for the balancing of the Trinity in each of the four lower bodies are transformed in the throat chakra into the sixteen aspects of virtues flowing in the

breath of the Holy Spirit. And behold, now there are
four petals in each of the four lower bodies! This tells
you that the threefold flame in etheric, mental,
emotional, and physical quadrants has become the
fourfold action of the law. The triangle has become
the square; and Spirit's flame is now ensconced in
Matter through the original decree of Alpha, "Let
there be light!" and the response of Omega, "And there
was light!"[17] And lo, the womb of creation, the Cosmic
Egg, was the materialization of the God flame!

Learn, then, that by the action of your word, all
that you garner in the chamber of the heart—the
wisdom and the love of the guru and the will of the
law—is sent forth as the *sword* of the sacred Word
to coalesce in Matter both the personality and the
patterns of the Infinite One. How the demons attack
the descent of the Word into form! What a blessing
when the Word *is* made flesh!

Take care, then, that you refrain from misusing
this sacred chakra that is the mouth of God. For is it
not written that "every idle word that men shall speak,
they shall give account thereof in the day of judgment;
for by thy words thou shalt be justified and by thy
words thou shalt be condemned"?[18] When you speak
the word in righteousness and love, the energy of
the heart flows with God-control to bless other parts
of life. When you speak unrighteousness and allow
the demons to mouth their unutterable mutterings
through you because you have confused the image of
the Holy One with that of the unholy one, then you
distort the pattern of the City Foursquare, you
unbalance the energies of life, and the grid of the new
dimensions which we seek to align with your aura is
broken and there is a shattering of crystal patterns as
the crystal-fire mist is dissipated in time and space.

Those who maintain the steady flow of the
compassionate word, the gentle word, speaking the

firmness of the law as it relates to the evolving soul consciousness, are those who overcome the accuser of the brethren by the blood of the Lamb—the essence of fire flowing from the heart chakra—and by the word of their testimony [19]—the release of that fire in the flowing water of the Word. As you then go forth to speak the word of truth, know that by the confirming of the Word with signs following [20] you build the kingdom of God on earth while laying up for yourselves treasure in heaven; [21] and the spiral of the aura expands with each affirmation of the law, each decree—each fiat of the Word.

As the pink is the glow of love that expands from the heart, so the blue is the ray of God's will that amplifies each expression of the law, each word of praise, and is the authority for healing and science in this octave. And if in the depths of darkest night the tempter would tempt you to doubt the power of the spoken Word as it is released through the omnipotent personality of the Godhead, remember then the one who appeared to John the Beloved in the midst of the seven candlesticks—"one like unto the Son of man, clothed with a garment down to the foot and girt about the paps with a golden girdle. His head and his hairs were white like wool, as white as snow; and his eyes were as a flame of fire; and his feet like unto fine brass, as if they burned in a furnace; and his voice as the sound of many waters. And he had in his right hand seven stars: *and out of his mouth went a sharp twoedged sword* [sacred word]: and his countenance was as the sun shineth in his strength." [22]

And know, then, that the Lord God himself is able to appear to the exalted consciousness of man and to proclaim to him directly by the power of the spoken Word: "Fear not; I AM the first and the last: I AM he that liveth and was dead; and, behold, I AM alive for evermore, Amen, and have the keys of hell and of death." [23]

This, my beloved, is the Impersonal Impersonality, the Impersonal Personality, the Personal Personality, and the Personal Impersonality which you can and shall become right within your forcefield, right within your aura, through the mastery of the power of the spoken Word.

I AM forever in the center of the flame,

Djwal Kul

VII

The Law of Congruency

Beloved Ones Who Stand to Make the Human Aura
                Congruent with the Divine:
      Understand that there are surrounding the body
of man concentric forcefields as envelopes within
envelopes; these are energy molds that determine the
quotient of light that can be contained within the
human aura. Just as the causal body consists of spheres
of light surrounding the Presence, each sphere noted
by a certain frequency depicted as a ring of color, so
around the body of man, lines of flux indicate layers of
frequencies which can be magnetized as you expand
your awareness of God.

      Beginning at the point in the center of the heart,
concentric rings of fire can be expanded in the aura of
the initiate who pursues the Presence of the Flaming
One. As the I AM Presence releases the light of God in
man, these energies expand outward from the heart in
ever-expanding rings like those that form when a
pebble is thrown into a pond. The soul that descends
into the planes of Matter has then the potential to be a
point of contact for solar hierarchies; for inherent
within the soul's own energy field are the electronic

matrices that enable it to become a center for the distribution of the light that is needed to nourish and sustain a planet and its evolutions.

Now as you read my words, sitting in meditation perhaps before the statue of the Buddha, the image of the Christ, or the Chart of Your Divine Self, visualize these concentric rings of light emanating from the center of your heart and realize that each successive attainment in cosmic consciousness anchors the light of the Cosmic Christ as a permanent layer of light within your aura. The layers of the aura that are filled with light mark the levels of initiation—of the neophyte, the postulant, the acolyte, the disciple, the adept, and so on in the hierarchical scale. When each layer is filled with light and the soul moves in its expanding self-awareness to the point where it magnetizes more light than the capacity of the layers, the aura is translated from the human to the divine; and it is not long before the soul is elevated in its expression from the planes of Matter to the planes of Spirit—for the world can no longer contain it.

As you increase the intensity of the aura through meditation and application of the sacred fire by giving mantras of the Spirit such as the Transfiguring Affirmations of Jesus the Christ,[1] which he taught to his disciples, you not only increase the dimensions of your aura in time and space, but you find that your aura becomes a means of communicating with new dimensions of the Spirit even while it transports your soul into higher frequencies of Matter.

Whereas your communication with beings and energies in the planes of Spirit may occur in periods of meditation and invocation, soul travel occurs most often while your body temple is at rest during the hours of sleep. For, you see, the aura that you build as a reflection of your awareness of God in many planes surrounds not only the physical form, but also the

etheric, mental, and emotional vehicles. The aura
then serves as the forcefield of light that has been
called the seamless garment. This garment adorns the
etheric body as that body becomes the vehicle of the
soul in its journeying in other octaves of Matter.

To develop the aura, then, is to prepare the place
of consciousness where, by the law of congruency, you
can receive here and now in the planes of Mater those
ascended masters and Christed ones whose light bodies
will mesh with your own because your aura has taken
on and become the frequency of the Holy Spirit that is
individualized by various members of the Great White
Brotherhood. To be sure, it is the dimensions of life
with which you identify whereby the attainment of
your cosmic consciousness is measured.

The action of the law of congruency is indeed
wondrous to behold! As the magnet of the heart in its
rising action is the equilateral triangle that compels
the descent of the triangle of Spirit, so that very six-
pointed star will magnetize to your heart an identical
momentum of light that is held in the heart of one or
more ascended beings.

By your free will you can qualify the interlaced
triangles of the heart with any of the frequencies of the
seven rays or of the Holy Ghost that is the unifying
Spirit of the Great White Brotherhood. When, for
instance, you dedicate the fires of your heart to the
Divine Mother and diligently give the salutations to
Mary,[2] your heart becomes an orifice of the Mother's
love, your aura contains the very patterns that flow
from the Virgin Queen to your own over the arc of
your adoration. At a certain point in your devotions
and in the evolution of your solar awareness of the
Divine Mother, the magnet of the aura and the heart
reaches, as it were, a critical mass — that is, an energy
momentum sufficient to magnetize the very living
Presence of the Divine Mother herself. And by the law

of congruency, your aura then becomes the aura of the
Virgin Mary.

Then as you recite the Hail Mary, you are giving
the salutation to the flame of the Divine Mother that
now burns within your own heart. And as you have
called to become her hands and her feet, her body and
her mind, so the call has compelled the answer and
the answer has come not as a miracle—not as an
exception to natural law, but in fulfillment of that law.
Thus as you increase the intensity and the light
frequency of the heart, which in turn feeds energy to
all of the chakras in Matter and expands the rings of
the aura, you come to the place where, through the
merging of the aura of the ascended masters with your
own, you can proclaim the joy of God's geometry;
"Behold, I and my Father are one, I and my Mother
are one!" And lo, the star above has become the star
below!

Wherever you are in consciousness at this moment, know, O chela of the light, that you are one with
every other soul, whether in Matter or in Spirit, who
is at this moment experiencing that level, that frequency, of God's being. If you are meditating upon
Jesus the Christ and his great life example, then you
are one with all others who have an identical appre-
ciation for his ministry. And if by your meditation
upon Jesus you become that Christ, then you are also
one with every other soul who has ever become the
Christ — past, present, and future.

No matter where you are or what you are doing,
you cannot escape the inevitable law of congruency.
If you allow yourself to become angered, willful,
rebellious, or entangled in the threads of maya, then so
long as you sustain that vibration by your free will, you
are one with and you reinforce the consciousness of all
others who are similarly preoccupied with the mists of
mortality. And the soul's apparatus to be a distributing

center for light is used to proliferate the energy veil, and the light that is in thee is darkness.[3]

When you consider the state of your mind and your feelings at any hour of the day or night, consider whether or not you would desire to have your aura amplify that state a million times, and consider whether you would have that state reinforced by other millions of auras which reflect your own and project the images of their consciousness upon the screen of the cosmos. Consider that your aura is a mirror of forces both within the microcosm of your individual world and within the entire macrocosm.

Consider that you, in your determination to focus a particular virtue of the Godhead, a certain aspect of the Holy Spirit, by the very intensity of your determination can magnetize the determination of God to be that virtue, that aspect. Therefore by maximizing the sacred fire within your heart through invocation, you can increase the concentric rings of influence that make up your aura. You can make your vote for light and for right count across the entire planetary body as your aura becomes a sounding board for the honor flame of ascended masters and cosmic beings whose light emanations are drawn by the very purity of your love and your determination to be a component of the divine consciousness.

Consider the enormous power of influence that you wield when you align yourself with cosmic forces and cosmic principles. And this is another key in understanding the simple statement "One with God is a majority." Consider also how your indulgences in the petulance and the pettiness of the ego reinforce the myopic existence of mankind who pursue an endless round of ego-centered activities and use their auras to amplify the ego personality of the synthetic image instead of the Christed personality of the Real Image.

When a man or a woman comes to the place

where he realizes the enormous responsibility of influencing life for good or for evil, he begins to understand the statement written in the law "I have said, Ye are gods."[4] Surely the power that a man can wield through the correct or the incorrect use of the aura can make of him instantaneously a god or a devil. The more you learn of the science of the aura, the more you will come to realize that there is no in-between; for every erg of energy and every microbe of thought, every wave of feeling, by the law of congruency and the oneness of all life in all planes, resounds throughout the creation either to increase or to decrease the light momentum of the aura of the cosmos.

Because of mankind's gross misuse of the power of the human aura in past ages, this power was taken from him by divine decree; the scientific and mathematical formulae for the development of the powers of the aura were withdrawn from the masses, and mankind's sensory and extrasensory perceptions became dulled according to their misuses of the powers of the aura. Finally, as abuses led to density and density to further abuses, even the knowledge of the existence of the aura was withdrawn. No longer having empirical proof of the existence of the aura, mankind, excepting the few, ceased to experiment with the science of auric emanations and control; and the soul's conquest of other dimensions of Matter that can be accomplished only through this science came to a halt.

In recent years, through Kirlian photography and experiments with plants, scientists have postulated the theory of the L-field as the blueprint of life and a forcefield of energy which can be observed and photographed with either scientific instruments or this specialized photography which uses neither camera nor lens. Suddenly now, after thousands of years of blindness and of the blind following the blind,

mankind have awakened to new planes of Matter
that exist and can be verified just beyond concrete
Matter. What a vast area of exploration and discovery experiments in parapsychology have opened, and
mankind are once again pushing back the frontiers of
knowledge! Hierarchy would provide extraordinary
insight into the delvings of scientists, and especially
those who are in fields of research that probe beyond
the present bounds of finite existence.

Man is on the brink of discovering the Higher
Self. His head peeping above the clouds, he beholds
himself alone against the backdrop of infinity. Beyond
mortality man must have the courage to proceed
alone — in the understanding that he is here and now
all one with life. In the stillness of the dawn man meets
the Infinite. As the last stars are put to bed and the
morning light quickens his solar awareness, man gazes
into the infinite blue; and he is aware that by the
power of an inner sight, a faculty of the soul, he is
contacting dimensions beyond the contemporary world
and beyond the knowledge of that world as man has
counted knowledge for thousands of years.

What is this infinite blue that the soul of man can
inhabit by simply expanding the faculties of soul? Is it
not the aura of God in the Macrocosm? As you
contemplate the self all one with the Higher Self
moving through the being of God, won't you give this
my prayer for the oneness of all life?

> O Infinite One,
> Thou God of all above, below,
> It is thyself that I would know.
> Come unto me, come into me,
> O God of love!
> Let me dwell with thee, in thee.
>
> My soul longs to climb the ladder of thy law.
> As children play on the playground

in their jungle gym,
So I would move along the parallel bars
    of thy congruency,
Of thy formlessness and form.
I would exercise my soul
Along the grids and forcefields
Of the antahkarana of life.
O God, let me feel
The rods and cones
That compose thy being.
For thou knowest, O God,
That I would heal
All those who have made themselves
Exceptions to thy law of congruency.

O God, how I love thy geometry
In time and space!
How I love thy design, thy creativity,
Thy bountiful grace!
O God, let me come home,
Let me tarry in the threefold essence
Of thy throne.

Ah yes, I would work thy works on earth
According to thy law —
Sacred wonder, sacred awe.
But for a moment, Lord,
Let me tarry in thy Word,
Let me come and kneel before thy throne.
Oh, let me sit at thy feet,
Divine Master, in thy retreat,
That I might renew the sacred essence
And the memory I once knew
Of our togetherness in the foreverness
Of the infinity I would view.

O God, as thou art
The point of light within my heart,

Let me enter there,
Let my soul be washed by flowing flame,
Let me be renewed to serve mankind again.
I am thy servant, Lord!
I am thyself in form, O Lord!
O Formless One, make us one,
That I might be the fullness of thyself
In and out of immortality.

Thy law is love, thy Word is truth.
Now let my soul be living proof
As thou art here and everywhere,
So I affirm I AM here and I AM there.
This then is the humble prayer
Of one who would become
The fullness of thy blazing Son.
I AM the oneness that I AM!

In the fullness of his love, I bid you welcome to my
aura. Will you welcome me to your aura?

I AM

Djwal Kul

VIII

The Sacred Fire Breath

To Those Who Would Pursue the Holy Spirit
        as the Sacred Fire Breath:
    As the inbreathing and the outbreathing of God is
for the integration of cosmic cycles, for the sending-
forth of worlds within worlds, and for the return of
those worlds back to the heart of God whence they
came, so man, as a co-creator with God, is endowed
with the gift of the sacred fire breath. And if he will
use that breath for the consecration of the energy of
the Holy Spirit within the chakras and within the aura,
he will find himself becoming the very fullness of the
Presence of God.
    How can this be? you say; for the mortal mind is
astounded at the very thought of being the expression
of God. Indeed, O mortal, thou canst not contain
immortality! Therefore, put off thy mortality! Enter in
to the consciousness of the immortals and know that
your aura can be, indeed now is, the very living
Presence of God—God as life pulsating, God as love
innovating, God as truth energizing the soul to the
fullness of its creative potential.
    The very air that you breathe can be qualified

with the sacred fire breath of the Holy Spirit. Indeed, the air is, as it were, the latent potential of the breath of the Holy Spirit. It is energy that is passive which can be activated by the Christ flame as the energy of the heart is drawn up through the throat chakra and released as the sacred Word.

Now we come to the great indrawing. Now we come to the place where — through unswerving devotion to the Son, through the conviction to be the Christ, and through the commitment to the Holy One and the name I AM THAT I AM — you have, in the flaming potential of being itself, the opportunity to become a spiral of integration in order that the life of God as Spirit might be integrated in Matter "as above, so below."

Understand, then, that by your application to the law that I have released in the first seven of these studies, there is being builded within your aura a fiery coil of life. This coil, which is approximately ten inches in diameter, you ought now to visualize rising from the base of an imaginary sundial upon which you stand. As you look down at your feet, the coil proceeds from what would be the twelve o'clock line (positioned just in front of your feet). The coil is an electrode that winds in a clockwise direction, the coils being spaced three inches apart. From beneath your feet to the top of your head, this coil is a pulsating white fire; and it can be focused as the action of the sacred fire of the Holy Spirit only in the aura of those who have the devotion to the Christ and the commitment to the I AM THAT I AM.

Retaining in mind and in heart the image and the awareness of this coil, let us now consider the two most important functions of the chakras: first, to be the vortex of the outbreath that is the giving-forth of God's energy as the action — the sevenfold activation — of the seven rays of the Holy Spirit; and second, to be the vortex of the inbreath, the drawing-in of the sacred fire breath as the universal essence, the passive energy of the Holy Spirit. These functions are most obvious in the throat chakra; and therefore the purpose of this eighth study in the series is to give the devotees of the Holy Spirit a truly practical exercise and a fundamental understanding of the use of the throat chakra for the integration of the four lower bodies through the inbreathing and outbreathing of the sacred fire breath.

Just as you breathe in and breathe out through the throat chakra, so all of the chakras are taking in and giving forth the energies of God according to the frequency assigned to each specific chakra. As the energies that are drawn in through the chakras are of the Holy Spirit and the Mother and relate to the functions of the soul in Matter and the nourishment of the four lower bodies, so the energies that are sent forth from the chakras are of the Father and the Son and relate to the functions of the soul in Spirit and the release of its spiritually creative potential.

In the ordinary, undeveloped man and woman, the interaction of these energies is sustained at mini-mum levels necessary for the flow, the harmony, and the nourishment of the four lower bodies. When man and woman, through a superior devotion and an extraordinary commitment to the Father and to the Son, begin to release a greater momentum of the energy of the Impersonal Impersonality and the Impersonal Personality of the Godhead through the chakras, then by this greater thrust of outflow there is magnetized a greater inflow of the Personal Per-sonality and the Personal Impersonality of the ener-gies of the Mother and of the Holy Spirit.

This is an illustration of the mathematical equa-tion that is always present in the cosmic exchange of energy from God to man and man to God. There-

fore balance, you see, is the key to the expansion
of the aura — and it is the balance of plus and minus
energy factors that is all important; for the aura will
expand in proportion as you increase both the velocity
and the vibration of energy moving into and coming
forth from the seven chakras of being. You who have
been diligent in studying our instruction and who have
made of that instruction the foundation of a new
dimension in consciousness will find that you have
already increased the outbreath — the outward thrust
of Spirit, the plus factor. The following exercise will
enable you to increase the inbreath — the inward thrust
of Mater, the minus factor. And so you will come to
know the balance of both as the regenerative action of
the currents of Alpha and Omega within your form
and consciousness and world.

First, place yourself in a meditative posture,
sitting in a comfortable chair before your altar, the
physical focus of your worship. If possible, you should
set aside a chair that is used only during your
meditations and invocations. You should consecrate
this chair by the momentum of your heart flame as a
focus of the atomic accelerator that is used by the
ascended masters in the Cave of Symbols. Chelas who
have passed certain initiations are bidden to sit in the
atomic accelerator to have the atoms and molecules of
the four lower bodies stepped up by the currents of the
ascension flame in preparation for the ritual of the
return, the alchemical marriage that is the soul's
reunion with the Spirit. Place your feet flat on the
floor, your hands cupped in your lap, your head erect,
eyes level, chin drawn in for the disciplined flow of the
energies of the heart through the throat chakra.

The Call to the Fire Breath, the invocation of the
Goddess of Purity given to the devotees of the Holy
Spirit, should now be recited three times.[1] Give it
slowly, rhythmically, with feeling. Absorb each word

and each concept with the conviction held in heart and mind that you are here and now a joint heir with Christ.[2] And as the beloved son, the beloved daughter, you are claiming your inheritance. Yours is an inheritance of the sacred fire that issues forth from the heart of beloved Alpha and Omega, who keep the flame of the Father-Mother God in the Great Central Sun.

The immaculate concept, the fiery blueprint according to which your soul was created in the image of the Divine One, is now impressed upon your four lower bodies. This fiery blueprint is magnetized by the coil described earlier in this lesson, which you now bring to the fore of consciousness as the pivot of your call to the fire breath. The fullness of the joy which you claim is the fullness of the expression of divine love. Now visualize the buoyant energies of love being magnetized by this coil and by the energies of the heart (which from our previous exercises you hold in mind as the focus of the interlaced triangles superimposed with the name of God).

It is essential that you hang above your altar the Chart of the Presence. Your eye level when you are standing should be at the eye level of the lower figure in the chart, so that the Christ Self and the I AM Presence are above you. Therefore, in all of your meditations and invocations, you should imagine through the imaging of the eye[3] that all energy released through the chakras comes forth from the I AM Presence, through the Christ Self, descending over the crystal cord into the heart chakra, thence throughout the four lower bodies.

Establish in mind, then, the concept of a perpetual flow from the heart of the individualized God Self to the heart of the Christ Self to your own threefold flame pulsating in the rhythm of God's heartbeat. The sealing of your aura within the very heart of the expanding fire breath of God is accomplished by your I AM Presence through the Christ Self in answer to your call. Remember, it is God in you who is the decreer, the decree, and the fulfillment of the decree.

Visualize your aura as an ovoid of white light extending beneath your feet, beneath the coil, above your head, and above the coil. See the aura increasing in the intensity of the light as that energy is expanded from the heart chakra and thence from all of the chakras as the sacred mist that is called the fire breath of God. Let its purity, wholeness, and love fill the ovoid of your aura; and feel your mind and heart disciplining that energy and holding it in the creative tension of your cosmic awareness. Conclude the giving of the call (three times) with the acceptance.

Now you are ready for the exercise of the integration of the eighth ray. To the count of eight beats, draw in through your nostrils the sacred breath. When you first begin this exercise, you may wish to count the eight beats by the gentle tapping of your foot. The breath is drawn in through the nostrils as you fill first the belly and then the lungs with air. Let your diaphragm be inflated like a balloon, and see the air that you draw in as the pure white light.

Now to the count of eight beats, hold in the air and visualize it penetrating your physical form as the essence of the Holy Spirit which nourishes, stabilizes, and balances the interchange of energy in the physical atoms, molecules, and cells. Visualize this sacred energy flowing through your veins, moving through your nervous system, anchoring the essence of the balancing energies of the Holy Spirit in your form, and absorbing from your form all impurities which you now see being flushed out of your system as you exhale to the count of eight beats.

Let the exhalation be deliberate and disciplined

as you slowly release the air as though it were a substance being pressed out of a tube. You may round your lips to increase the tension of the exhalation. See and feel that breath being pushed out from the very pit of the stomach. You may lean forward if this helps to press out the last bit of air remaining in the diaphragm. Now let your head resume an erect posture, and hold without inbreathing or outbreathing to the final count of eight beats.

Repeat this exercise daily, as you are physically able, until you have established a rhythm—mentally counting, if you wish, "One and two and three and four and five and six and seven and eight and one and two and three and"—and so forth. Be careful that in your zeal you do not overdo. Each one must in Christ discern his capacity, which may be anywhere from one to twelve repetitions of the exercise per daily session.

This fourfold exercise is for the balancing of the four lower bodies. The inbreath comes through the etheric body; the first hold is an action of energizing through the mental body; the outbreath is the release through the emotional body; and the final hold is for the anchoring in the physical form of the balanced action of Father, Son, Mother, and Holy Spirit.

When you have mastered the inbreathing, holding, outbreathing, and holding in this fashion and the accompanying visualization of the sacred fire releasing light, energizing the consciousness, extracting impurities, and finally anchoring the energies of the Christ, then—and only then—you may add to your exercise the affirmation "I AM Alpha and Omega" to the count of eight beats. This you mentally affirm once for each of the four steps of the exercise. This affirmation is for the establishment within you of the cloven tongues of fire, the twin flames of the Holy Spirit that are the energies of the Father-Mother God.

By thus invoking these energies and using the

breath as the means to convey that energy to the four lower bodies and to anchor it in the physical form, you will be building the balanced action of the caduceus — the intertwining of the Alpha and Omega spirals along the spine that are for the ultimate victory of the masculine and feminine polarity that raises the energies of the chakras, merges in the heart as the Christ, and flowers in the crown as the Buddhic enlightenment of the thousand-petaled lotus.

Since the Fall of Man, mankind have allowed the energies of the four lower bodies to remain in a state of imbalance. Therefore, they have not had the equal flow of the currents of Alpha and Omega anchored within their forms which are necessary to sustain the currents of regeneration, of eternal youth, and above all, to expand the aura to planetary and interplanetary dimensions. As a result, the unnatural law of sin, disease, decay, and death has displaced the natural law of harmony in the evolutions of earth.

Without the balance of the spirals of Alpha and Omega within you, O chelas of the sacred fire, you can go no further in the expansion of the aura. All that we have given thus far is a foundation upon which you may now build the consciousness of the Father-Mother God. And as you increase that balance through this exercise day by day, you will come in to the awareness that you are indeed the beloved of God and that in you is the converging in the planes of Mater of the twin flames of Alpha and Omega.

Behold, "I AM Alpha and Omega, the beginning and the ending, saith the Lord, which is, and which was, and which is to come, the Almighty."[4] This, then, is the beginning of your exercise of expansion. It is also the ending of your exercise; for ultimately in the completed manifestation of the Father-Mother God, you will find that your being and consciousness has become the aura, the forcefield, of the Holy Spirit.

You will find that you have thereby magnetized that Presence of the I AM and that you are magnetized by it in a literal conflagration which is, blessed ones, the ritual of your ascension in the light. Thus from beginning to ending, the Alpha and Omega spirals within you are the fulfillment of the very living Presence of God.

I place my Electronic Presence with each one as the guardian action of the sacred fire — I AM the guard — during the period of your meditation on the fire breath and your exercise of integration through the eighth ray.

I AM the willing servant of the flame,

Djwal Kul

IX

The Mastery of the Four Elements
in the Planes of the Chakras

To Those Who Would Flow
    with the Sacred Fire Breath:
    In order to master the flow of God's energy
through the seven chakras, man and woman ought to
consider the mastery of the four elements—of fire, air,
water, and earth—as planes of God's consciousness.
For by the mastery of the four elements, you will then
gain the mastery of the flow of energy through the four
lower bodies as these bodies serve as coordinates for the
establishment of the aura of God around the soul.
    The four elements, so-called, are merely word
matrices used to define the planes of God's Self-
awareness which the individual is capable of realizing
through the four lower bodies. Thus the etheric body is
the vehicle for the fire element and for man's realization of God's awareness of himself as the sacred
fire. The highest frequencies which the individual is
capable of realizing in the planes of Mater are focused
through this body. The etheric or memory body
contains both the record of the soul's evolution in the
causal body in the planes of Spirit prior to its descent
into Mater and the record of all of its experiences in

the lower octaves after the descent.

It is through the heart chakra, where the ascending and descending triangles converge, that the soul learns to exercise the sacred fire and its uses both in the planes of Spirit and in the planes of Mater. By the fire of the heart, man and woman learn the mastery of the etheric cycles of the cosmos which spiral through the etheric body; and by the energies of the heart they do weave the deathless solar body—the body into which the etheric body is transformed once the karmic cycles have been fulfilled.

Thus our God who is a consuming fire [1] can be experienced in the planes of Mater through the heart chakra. And it is, of course, the threefold flame anchored therein that conveys this aspect of the mastery of the Christ consciousness to the Soul. Then by the mastery of this fire element, the disciple is able to magnetize greater and greater portions of the flame into the aura. The balanced manifestation of the fire element and the infilling of the aura with the fires of the Holy Ghost prepare the disciple for the mastery of the other six chakras through the mental, emotional, and physical bodies.

The air element and God's awareness of himself in the plane of the mind in and as the Logos are mastered in the mental body through the third eye and the seat-of-the-soul chakra. The frequency of this element is comparable to the wind that "bloweth where it listeth" [2] and to thinking and be-ness whereby the soul affirms "I am," as the expression of self-identity, drawing the conclusion "therefore I think"—or "I think, therefore I am."

For the mastery of the emotions—of God's awareness of himself as energy in *motion*—and of the water element, the disciple has the opportunity to expand and balance the energies of life and their flow in the emotional body (sometimes called the desire body) through the throat chakra and the solar plexus. But the full mastery of the physical plane and of time and space in Mater is not attained until the disciple gains the mastery of the flow of physical energies in the base-of-the-spine and the crown chakras.

In these two chakras the disciple experiences God's awareness of himself as Mother and Father united in the physical plane for the bringing-forth of the Christ consciousness. And thus the goal of the adepts of the East who meditate upon the Goddess Kundalini as the white-fire energies of the Mother coiled as the serpent fire in the base of the spine is to raise that energy through all of the chakras and to attain the merging of the energy of the Mother (which otherwise remains locked in the base of the spine) with those of the Father as these are quickened by the divine union of the Alpha-to-Omega spirals in the crown chakra.

Let us consider in this study the mastery of the flow of the sacred fire as it becomes in the throat chakra the waters of the living Word and in the solar plexus the peace-commanding Presence. Beloved Jesus, the Prince of Peace who was the Master of the Piscean age, set the example for all mankind's mastery of God's energies in motion. So great was his mastery of the flow of fire from the heart into these two chakras that he was able to proclaim, "Heaven and earth shall pass away, but my words shall not pass away."[3] By this he meant that even though the entire forcefield of the soul's identity in the planes of Mater, together with the chakras that are used to focus the energies of heaven and earth, might cease to exist, the word of God uttered through his being would remain forever—fixed as stars in the firmament of God's being.

The mark of the Christed one is the mark of attainment whereby the energies of the chakras below the heart are uplifted and integrated with the energies

The Seven Centers of God-Awareness

The seven centers in your being are for the release of God's energy. God's awareness of himself as love is anchored in your heart. God's awareness of himself as power is anchored in your throat, in the authority of the Word. God's awareness of himself as vision is anchored in your third eye. God's awareness of himself as wisdom is anchored in your crown. God's awareness of himself as peace is in the solar plexus. God's awareness of himself as freedom is in the seat of the soul. And God's awareness of himself as purity is in the base of the spine.

These seven centers are seven planes of consciousness. We experience God differently in different frequencies. We experience God as love in the heart and as our communication of love. We experience him as law and authority in the spoken Word and in its power. We experience him as vision, as seeing, as precipitation, as science and truth in the third eye. This experiencing of God enables us to become God, to know God, to be filled with God, and finally to put on, totally, the consciousness of God in the ritual of the ascension.

We cannot inherit immortality as mortals. The mortal must put off its mortality to become immortality. The mortal itself cannot be immortalized. It must be replaced. This is why Paul said that this corruptible must put on incorruption, that this mortal must put on immortality. And yet Paul said that flesh and blood cannot inherit the kingdom of God.

What, then, is worthy to inherit God? Only God is worthy of God. Unless we sense ourselves in and as God, we will not consider ourselves to be worthy of God. It is not our four lower bodies which can contain infinity. They are finite cups holding a portion of infinity while we move in time and space. But the centers of God-awareness are coordinates of infinity actually anchored in our body consciousness. Therefore, that which inherits immortal life is the immortal flow of God which we make our own through the chakras.

ECP

Plate 1

Chela Invoking the Violet Flame and Tube of Light. The soul stands in the violet flame invoking the violet fire. We need the violet flame to purify the tabernacle of our witness. The violet flame is necessary as an insulation and as a purifier. The tube of light is necessary because we are separating ourselves out from the mass consciousness programmed in the cult of death and dying, programmed in the laws of mortality and limitation.

This is where you now are. You are surrounded by sheaths of consciousness, the four lower bodies. You have the threefold flame within your heart. You have the halo of the Christ around you and you see the crystal cord of energy, God's energy descending to you every moment. That means that you have limitless power and limitless wisdom, limitless love at your command, if you will draw it forth and use it in the name of your own beloved Christ Self.

ECP

Plate 1

Plate 2

Heart Chakra. The most important chakra is the heart, for it is the distributing center for the energies of life. From the heart chakra—with its twelve petals surrounding the threefold flame of power, wisdom, and love held in the balance of the Christ consciousness—the energy from the Presence is distributed to the other six major chakras and to the five minor chakras, the chakras of the secret rays, thence to all of the cells and centers in the four lower bodies. Through the anchoring of the threefold flame within the heart, your heart is a replica of the heart of God and of the heart of Christ. The white-fire core out of which the flame springs forth is the wholeness of the Father-Mother God. The heart where the pink fires of love burn brightly is a replica of the Great Central Sun. When we maintain in the heart the frequency of the Christ out of compassion for all life, we find all life as one; for the threefold flame is at the heart of all life.

ECP

Plate 2

Plate 3

Throat Chakra. The throat chakra, which focuses sixteen petals of light, is the power center in man. The sixteen frequencies for the precipitation in the four planes of Mater correspond to the thought form of the pyramid—four petals on each side of the pyramid, on each side of the square—a very important mandala for the Word becoming flesh, for the Spirit becoming tangible in Matter.

This center of the blue ray of the will of God is the key to the shortening of the days for the elect that Jesus said would occur. The shortening of the days, or the cycles, of the balancing of karma occurs through the correct use of the spoken Word. When we use the name of God "I AM" and follow it with affirmations of light, we begin the transmutation process. Anything and everything that proceeds from the throat chakra coalesces in form, for good or for ill, by the action of the power of the Word.

ECP

Plate 3

Plate 4

Third-Eye Chakra. We return to the absolute consciousness of Good through the third-eye chakra, which has ninety-six petals. The third eye, vibrating in the emerald green of the science of truth, gives us the immaculate picture of individuals, of civilizations, of the divine pattern. Through this chakra you tune in to what should be in reality instead of what is happening or being outpictured in the actualities of the present. You can always tell whether or not you are looking through the third eye or through the two eyes: the third eye always gives you the immaculate concept of the blueprint of life as well as the discrimination to know good and evil.

ECP

Plate 4

Plate 5

Crown Chakra. It is in the crown that man is destined to focus the consciousness of God. The crown chakra is called the thousand-petaled lotus. It is a golden yellow and has 972 petals.

The goal of mastery in time and space is the flowering of the crown, which occurs when the energies of man's being, once he is perfected, rise for the expansion and the unfolding of the petals of the Lord's wisdom. When we attain to that crown consciousness, true wisdom is known. The true enlightenment of the Buddha and of the Christ that comes with that golden yellow fire on the crown is the experience of knowing all things without being tutored or taught. Our awareness then includes that which is contained in the mind of God.

ECP

Plate 5

Plate 6

Solar-Plexus Chakra. The solar plexus, the "place of the sun," is the place of feeling and the place where we employ the energy of emotion as God's energy in motion in order to focus the peace of God's consciousness, the peace of the ascended Jesus Christ. When your solar plexus is calm, you have the power of peace; and, using the full potential of the desire body, you have that full momentum of the "Pacific Ocean," of water molded in a matrix of love. This power of the purple and gold ray of God's desiring to be God comes forth as you raise the energy from the solar plexus to the level of the throat and release the fiat, as Jesus did, "Peace, be still!" Through that fiat, a wave of light goes over the whole planet, causing atoms and electrons to come into alignment with the flame of the Prince of Peace. The solar-plexus chakra has ten petals.

ECP

Plate 7

Seat-of-the-Soul Chakra. The seat-of-the-soul chakra is the place where the soul is anchored to the etheric and physical bodies. This is the chakra of freedom, of the fires of freedom, of the seventh ray of Saint Germain. It is the violet flame that liberates the soul from all perversions to become all that God has made it to be. The six petals of this chakra represent the six-pointed star of victory. They govern the flow of light and the karmic patterns in the genes and chromosomes and in the sperm and the egg of man and woman.

ECP

Plate 7

Plate 8

Base-of-the-Spine Chakra. The base-of-the-spine chakra, which has four petals, sets the pattern for the flowering of the Mother flame in the four lower bodies of man. This chakra is also the foundation of the physical body. Our entire physical body is a manifestation of Mother because it is Spirit's point of focalization in the material universe. It is from this point that man rises for the reunion of Mother with the Father in the crown, which brings forth the Christ in the center of the heart.

When you have the mastery of this chakra, you attain the consciousness of Mother Mary, of being omnipresent. And it is the energies of the power of the fourth ray through this chakra which give you the power to be everywhere on earth simultaneously.

ECP

Plate 8

Plate 9

Heart Chakra with I AM THAT I AM. The magnet that you create within the heart is the ascending triangle. And the more you meditate upon this triangle superimposed upon the heart, the more it becomes the reality of the dimensions of the Sacred Trinity in manifestation. As surely as the call compels the answer, so the presence of this forcefield, of this triangle, combined with the letters of living flame "I AM THAT I AM," will draw the descending triangle of God's consciousness into the heart. And this merging of Creator and creation through the intercession of the Christ Self and the Christ flame is the foundation of our exercise whereby the aura of man becomes the aura of God.

pages 28-29

Plate 9

Plate 10

Muddied Aura 1. This is an example of the completely uncontrolled release of energy in the thought and feeling world. This energy is not being spent in the perversion of sex; it is rather being raised and allowed to go through the third eye and the crown imperfectly. Because we have free will, we can do exactly what we will with the energies of the chakras.

Chakras have a yin and a yang action. They are for the release of the current of Alpha, or the masculine ray, into the world, filling our aura with Spirit, and they are for the taking-in of prana, or of the Holy Spirit, which is a feminine action. We are intended to simultaneously release God's light and take in God's light, release it as Father, take it in as Mother; and that is the balance of the T'ai chi in each chakra. It forms a basket-weave effect as the centers are whirling.

In this drawing you see the beginning of human creation. You can see the misuse of the spoken Word and the flame of blue descending as a tirade of energy. You can see the misuse of the heart chakra stirring up the emotions and the misuse of the base of the spine and the seat of the soul. There is a mental explosion going on in this person's consciousness. That mental explosion is the misuse of the third eye, the sending forth of images that are incorrect. This person is incorrectly qualifying all of the seven rays; and the crown, which should be the crown of life, is releasing nothing but the human consciousness, adding to the mass consciousness of the race.

ECP

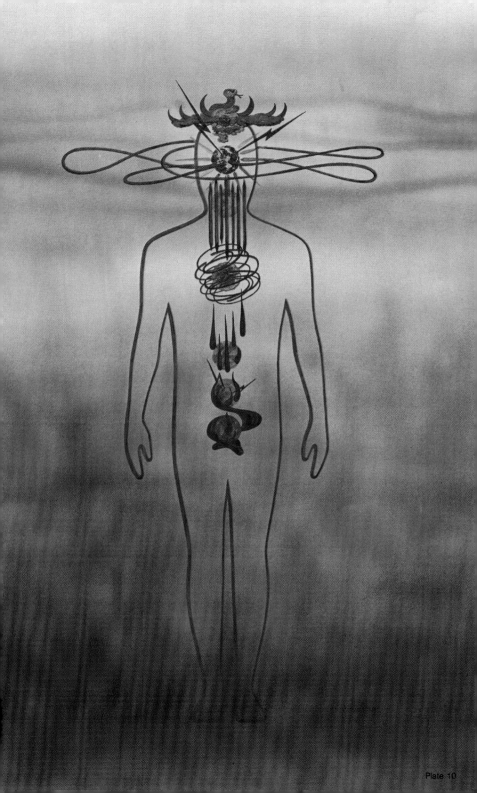

Plate 10

Plate 11

Muddied Aura 2. This is another form of misqualification filling the aura with brown. That sinking feeling you get in the
belly when you contact human creation sinks all of the energy
down, down, and down. These lines from the heart indicate a
very direct action of psychic consciousness coming out as a
psychic hook. A psychic hook hooks you into someone's
human consciousness through sympathy. The impure heart
colors all of the other chakras. It is dripping with human
sympathy that is going to affect the emotions, color the soul
and the soul awareness, and finally result in the misuse of the
base-of-the-spine chakra.

ECP

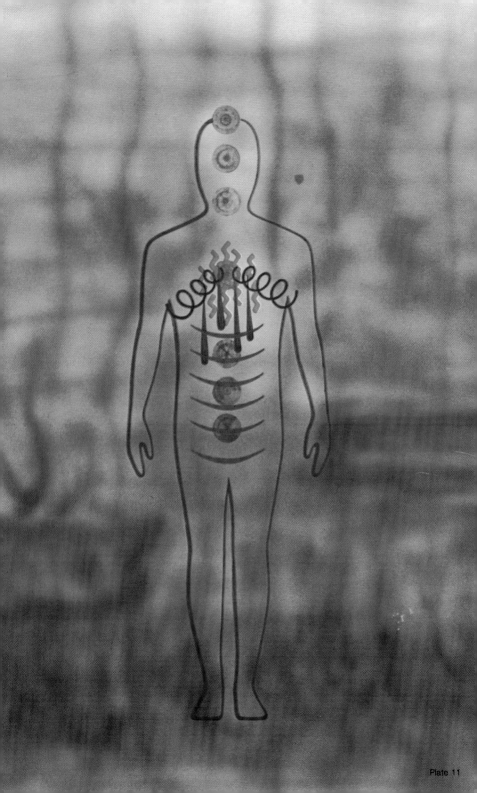

Plate 11

Plate 12

Muddied Aura 3. Here there is the centering of the misuse of the sacred fire in the crown and the third eye. This is the misqualification of someone who is mentally polarized and yet whose mind is not filled with the Christ consciousness. This person can be steeped in any kind of philosophy or carnal or intellectual accomplishment and yet he will not have the corona, the crown of the Christ, the halo of life. His crown and head area will be marked by this type of manifestation. While the other chakras are impure, most of the energy that this person receives from God is misqualified mentally. These are the people who are mentally polarized but not Christ-polarized.

ECP

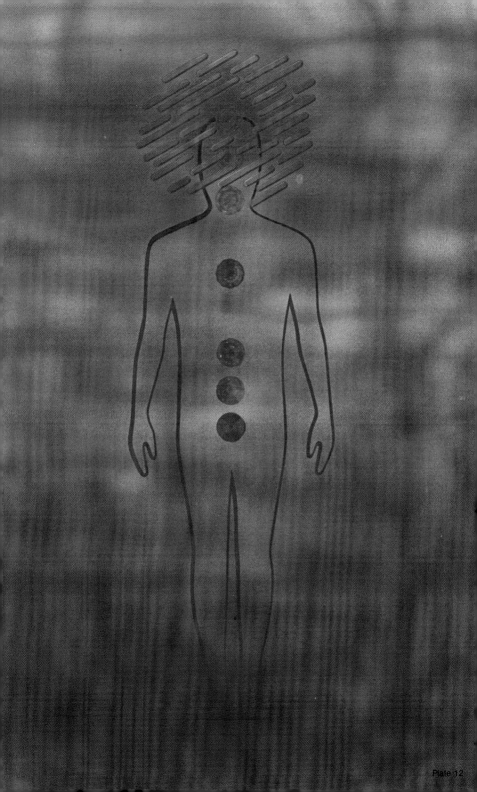

Plate 12

Plate 13

Muddied Aura 4. This is a typical aura of the mass consciousness. By the mass consciousness we mean the
collective unconscious of the mankind who move as one, the
sea of humanity who are not enlightened. Their auras will be
filled with the brown and green of the muck just like the muck
you see at the bottom of a river. They move in the astral plane.
They do not invoke the tube of light or the violet flame, and so
their auras simply take on and are colored by their surround-
ings.

The lines of red and orange show that these people are a
powder keg, that they are ready to become angry at the
moment that their egos are offended. The potential for anger is
there. Put them in contact with someone who is separated out
from the mass consciousness and they are likely to explode
because they cannot bear the contact with light. Put them in
contact with people who are part of the milling crowd, part of
the herd, and they get along just fine. They move in between
one another's angers and passions and prides, and they get
along and tolerate one another's human effluvia.

These people are largely dominated by what we call the
moon consciousness. The moon as an orange focal point or
cap completely obliterates the contact of God through the
crown chakra. The moon as a black focus of the crescent at
the base of the spine cuts off the contact with the Mother and
the purity of the flame. These people will be governed by the
cycles of the moon. As the moon goes through the twelve
houses, the twelve signs of the zodiac, each twenty-eight
days, they will tend to take on the misuses of God's energy
through lunar substance, which is the emotional misuse of the
sacred fire. This aura is typical of the man on the street.

ECP

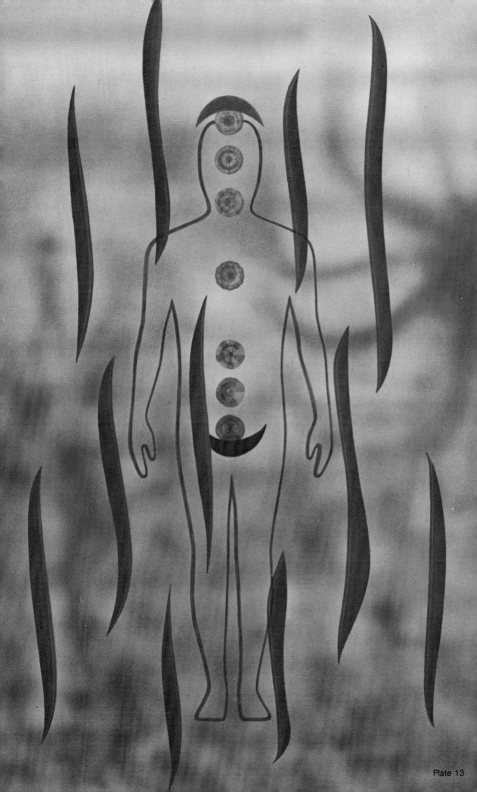

Plate 13

Plate 14

Muddied Aura 5. This is another action of the mass consciousness. The person has a considerable amount of faith. Notice the blue halo around his head. This might be a very religious person with a bit of illumination in the aura such as he can glean from his faith; but you'll notice that the heart is a sympathetic heart. The energies of the heart, instead of coming out in a direct line, are tending to fall, because this person has not discerned the difference between compassion and sympathy. This person is always in sympathy with someone who is the underdog, and the sympathy goes to the solar plexus.

This is the kind of person who is always identifying with someone's human creation. Instead of exalting the Christ, he sinks to the level of whoever he is with, whoever has a problem. Instead of using the light of the heart to uplift, to ennoble, to instill with the Christ awareness, he tends to use the heart energy to be "in agreement with"—which is what sympathy means—someone's human creation.

Now we will find that among mankind there are very sincere people; but because they do not have the Holy Spirit and its action, their auras have not been purged of this substance. As soon as they begin to use the violet flame, it will begin to disappear. Their chakras will be more aligned in their four lower bodies and we will find a more intense radiation—beginning as a trickle, then intensifying as a beacon light through all of the chakras.

This is how a very ordinary person—not particularly good, not particularly bad—might walk into a seminar on the teachings of the ascended masters. By the time he leaves that seminar in two days, he would have his aura bristling with the violet flame and this substance transmuted. Auras change very quickly. The moment this person comes in contact with the Holy Spirit, that quickening fire passing through will lift this substance and give him an entirely new awareness of God. But there are many layers of misqualified energy to be consumed, and the scrubbing action of the violet flame works both from the surface of the aura to the chakras and from the threefold flame within the heart chakra to the surface.

ECP

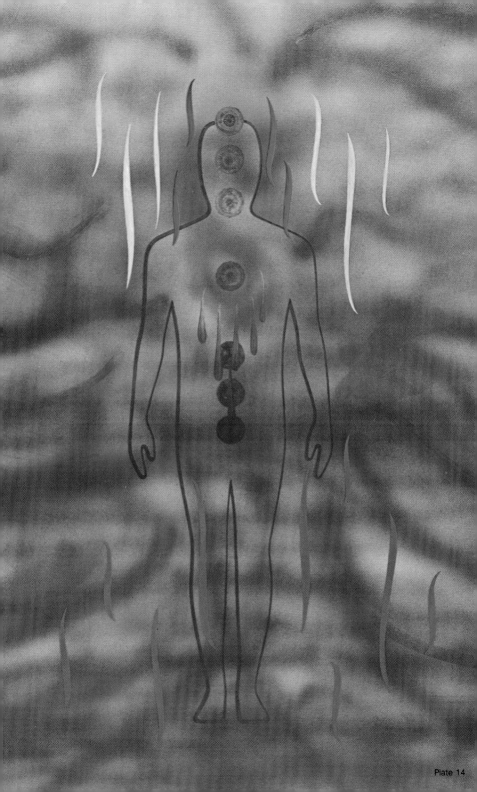

Plate 14

Plate 15

Muddied Aura 6. In this drawing we see a greater misuse of the sacred fire through the power of the spoken Word. This is mortal cursing; it is malice; it is being completely out of control in the throat chakra. It is sending forth arrows and barbs and psychic wedges. The red denotes the passion; the black denotes the total misuse of the Word of God. This person is in a state of anger, and I am certain you have seen these people even in public places. They become slightly irritated and they go into a tirade. They start swearing at the nearest person they think has done something wrong to them. They are polluting the aura of their own world and the aura of the earth.

This is pollution. This is where pollution starts. This is where we have to start cleaning up pollution. If you ever have a tantrum, this is what you look like. All of your chakras are discolored, but here you see what you are doing to the throat chakra. The beautiful flow of God's pure blue energy in the Word of God is desecrated and compromised beyond recognition.

This energy, of course will accumulate. When I say energy is transmuted quickly, I mean the surface and I mean the changing manifestation of the immediate aura. But the karma of the misuse of this energy settles. It settles in the electronic belt which surrounds the chakras below the heart, and that takes time to clean up. It takes meditation; it takes invocation; it takes the violet flame to clean up the residue of misqualified energy that does settle in the electronic belt. And so the immediate and surface vibration of the aura may be cleaned quickly, but the misuse of energy that piles up century after century takes certain cycles to clear.

ECP

Plate 15

Plate 16

Muddied Aura 7. This figure shows the aura of the black magician misusing the energies of the third eye and the solar plexus. You can see the demon forms, the demons of the mind that this individual is projecting to carry out his will. The person that I took this reading from is actually a figure well placed in our government; and that aura shows a master-minded manipulation of forces, of nations, and of the planet itself.

Now when we are confronted by this energy, how does it affect us? It can affect us as if we were hypnotized. Almost trembling, we feel that we are being totally subjugated by the intimidation of the fallen one. These people have an almost overpowering will of human personality. They put over their ideas, their policies—whatever they are going to put over— with an intense use of the third-eye chakra. They become so strong in their misuse of energy that it takes people who have a corresponding momentum of Christ consciousness in the same chakra to see through them and to overcome them.

Most people among humanity do not have this degree of misuse of the sacred fire, nor do they have its corresponding attainment in the Christ consciousness; so they become victimized by those who are black magicians. Until they attain a corresponding amount of the Christ consciousness, they are defenseless, except through invocation to the I AM Presence and the Christ Self, who will immediately overshadow the soul who is confronted by the "accuser of the brethren."

ECP

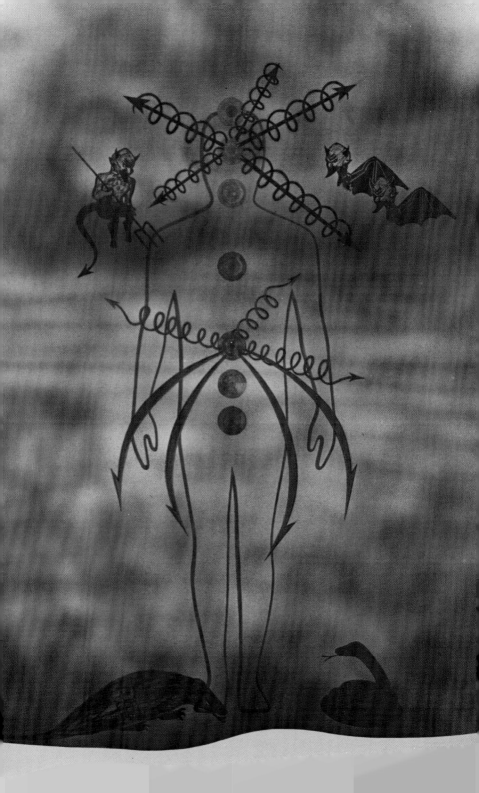

Plate 17

Muddied Aura 8. This drawing shows the total mechanization concept—an individual totally dominated by the mass mind. This is not unusual to see in the auras of people. You see that the kundalini is nothing but an orange coil rising from the base of the spine. All energy is misused in all of the chakras, putting out a net of materialism and mechanization—throat chakra misused, all of the chakras overdeveloped with the perversions of the seven rays. It is not pretty; but I assure you, this entire plane of the human consciousness is not pretty. This is what God, as the flame of life within, cleans up when we diligently invoke the sacred fire. The animal form indicates the animal magnetism and its calcification in the planes of the subconscious mind.

ECP

Plate 17

Plate 18

Chela Standing in the Ovoid. This plate shows the action of the sacred fire invoked as a replica of the Cosmic Egg sealing the pure energies flowing through purified chakras.

ECP

Visualize your aura as an ovoid of white light extending beneath your feet, beneath the coil, above your head, and above the coil. See the aura increasing in the intensity of the light as that energy is expanded from the heart chakra and thence from all of the chakras as the sacred mist that is called the fire breath of God. Let its purity, wholeness, and love fill the ovoid of your aura; and feel your mind and heart disciplining that energy and holding it in the creative tension of your cosmic awareness.

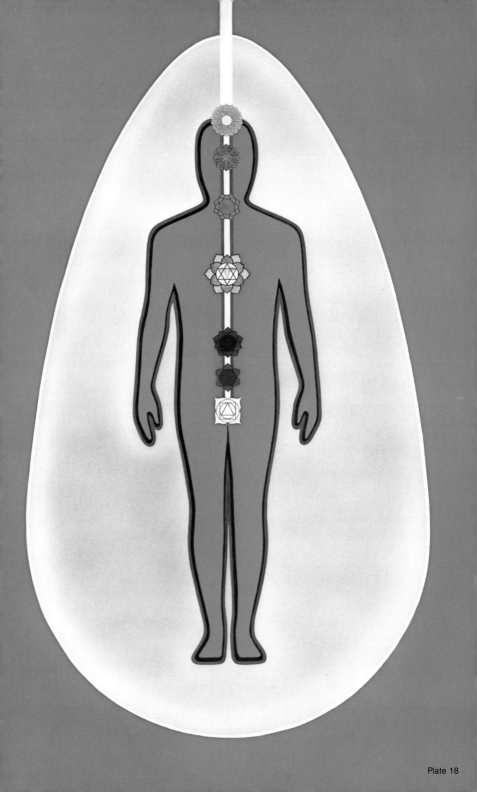

Plate 18

Plate 19

Caduceus Action through Purified Chakras. The four petals of the Mother are for the anchoring in Matter-form of the action of the squaring of the fires of the heart whereby the circle of infinity becomes the cube of God Self-awareness in time and space. The four petals form the base of the figure-eight pattern—even the flow of the caduceus—that crosses in the heart of man and reaches its culmination in the crown of life. These four petals symbolize twin flames mastering the energies of life "as above, so below"—plus and minus in Alpha, plus and minus in Omega. Whether in Spirit or in Mater, in the flame of the Divine Mother twin flames converge for the union of the energies of life that are for the emancipation of the Christ consciousness in all. White light bursts forth as a thousand suns signal across the skies the fohatic emanations of the eternal Logos.

pages 108-9

Plate 19

Plate 20

The Fiery Coil of Life. Understand, then, that by your application to the law that I have released in the first seven of these studies, there is being builded within your aura a fiery coil of life. This coil, which is approximately ten inches in diameter, you ought now to visualize rising from the base of an imaginary sundial upon which you stand. As you look down at your feet, the coil proceeds from what would be the twelve o'clock line (positioned just in front of your feet). The coil is an electrode that winds in a clockwise direction, the coils being spaced three inches apart. From beneath your feet to the top of your head, this coil is a pulsating white fire; and it can be focused as the action of the sacred fire of the Holy Spirit only in the aura of those who have the devotion to the Christ and the commitment to the I AM THAT I AM.

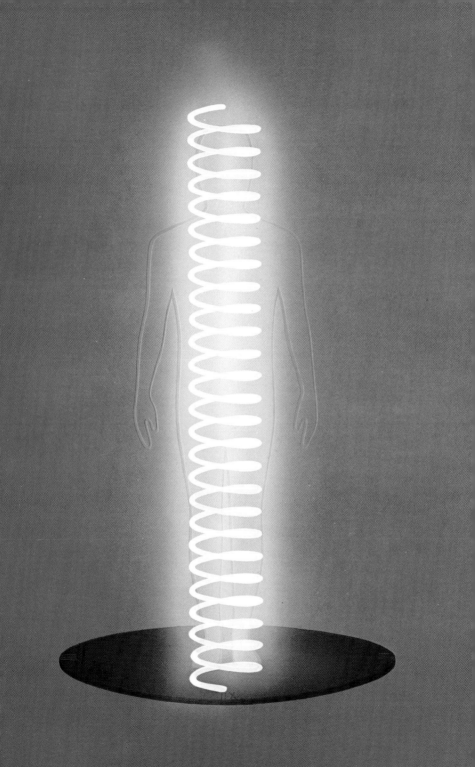

Plate 20

Plate 21

Individualization of the God Flame from out the Presence of the I AM THAT I AM in the Great Central Sun. In the heart there is a pulsation of life becoming life that is the established rhythm of the cosmos reflected from the heart of God to the heart of the Great Central Sun, through the heart of the Elohim, thence to all lifewaves evolving in time and space. The heart is the focal point for the flow of life individualized as the I AM Presence, the Divine Monad of individuality, the Christ Self that is the personification of the reality of being for every soul. The heart is the connecting point for all being, for all self-consciousness. Through the heart all mankind are one; and through the heart the Christ of the One, the only begotten Son of the Father-Mother God, becomes the Christ of all lifewaves unfolding God's life throughout the cosmos.

Plate 2

Plate 22

Concentric Rings Emanating from the Seven Chakras and from the Secondary Heart Chamber. We have described the rings of light which in the Christed ones are continually emanating from the heart chakra. Let us also consider that there is intended to be a continual release of concentric rings of light not only from the heart, but from all of the chakras. This release becomes possible as the individual consciously employs the chakras as distributing centers for the energies of the I AM Presence that circulate from the heart throughout the four lower bodies. Day by day as the aspirant gains control of the flow of life through his being, the inflow and the outflow of the life forces in the chakras increase until the hour of the transfiguration, when all of the seven chakras, together with the secondary heart chamber, are simultaneously releasing the color rings of the seven rays and the eighth ray from the base of the spine to the crown.

pages 83-84

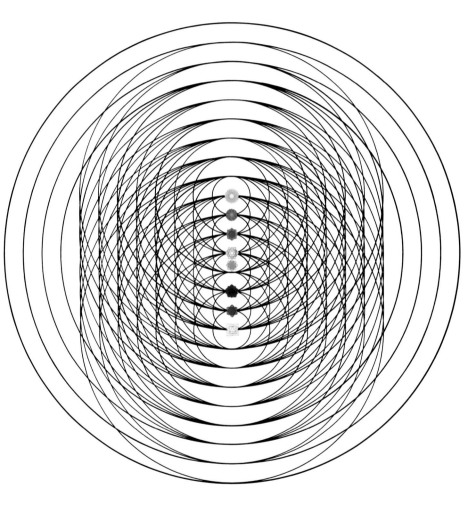

Plate 22

Plate 23

Meditation in the Pyramid of the Thirteen Steps of Initiation. The chela meditating in the pyramid is meditating on the thirteen steps of initiation in the Christ consciousness—the twelve initiations of the disciples on the twelve points of the cosmic clock and the initiations of the Christ consciousness in the center of the clock. These are illustrated by thirteen spirals, or levels of attainment, which are achieved through the seven chakras.   ECP

Thirty-Three Coils of Victory. The thirty-three cycles in the lower pyramid denote the thirty-three initiations on the path of the ascension successfully demonstrated by Jesus the Christ.

ECP

Every soul that would be free must accept the challenge to be the fullness of the law of life and the balance of the threefold flame in manifestation in each of the four lower bodies. And so you see, when the twelve godly attributes have been magnetized in the heart chakra, they can be squared through the vision of the all-seeing eye of God in the third-eye chakra. And when the threefold flame and the twelve virtues are balanced in the four lower bodies, there is the converging of energy spirals in the third eye as the capstone is placed on the pyramid of life in the coming of the Christ consciousness.

page 100

Plate 24

Transfiguration of the Son of God. It was love as he lived and breathed the essence of the Holy Spirit which paved the way for mastery in the life of Jesus, a way which became a spiral of ascending currents of love over which the soul fulfilled its immortal destiny, being received in a cloud of love, the forcefield of his very own I AM Presence.

Through the threefold flame within the heart, the threefold nature of God is realized in man and in woman. How clear is the word of the Lord throughout the ages! Two thousand years ago and throughout an eternity before and after, the law remains. To love God with all thy heart is to attain his Christ consciousness; to love God with all thy soul is to attain his soul consciousness; to love God with all thy mind is to attain his God consciousness.

pages 16-17

Plate 23

Plate 24

of the chakras above the heart. Those above the heart carry the masculine polarity of being, and those below the heart carry the feminine polarity. Once the energies of the heart are balanced in and as the threefold flame, then the individual can proceed to balance the other six chakras — each chakra being one of the points on the two interlaced triangles necessary for the attainment of the Christ consciousness.

Jesus is known as the Prince of Peace because he balanced the threefold flame in the heart and mastered the flow of the sixth ray, the energies of purple and gold in the solar plexus chakra (at the navel). Holding these energies in harmony, he was able as the occasion arose to draw upon the reserves locked in the solar plexus chakra and to release this energy in and as the power of the spoken Word. It was, then, in the perfect balance of the flow from the desire body, which in Jesus totally reflected God's desiring for mankind, that he was able to speak the word of healing, of forgiveness, of comfort, that he was able to give forth the teaching of the Christ for the Piscean age and to speak the word that raised the dead, cast out the demons, and aligned the entire planetary body with the aura of the Christ. (Of course all of his chakras were in the perfect balance of the Star of David.)

You may then visualize the ascending triangle of purple flecked with gold rising from the solar plexus and merging in the throat chakra with the descending triangle of royal blue for the fulfillment of the spirals of Alpha and Omega in the release of the spoken Word. These color rays, the blue and the purple, do focus the action of the beginning and the ending that seals the sacred fire breath in a matrix of completion specifically for precipitation in Mater. When the energies in motion of these two chakras are perfectly balanced, then when the disciple speaks the word "Be

thou made whole!" it is done, even as the fiat of the
Lord spoken by Jesus was a rebuke to the devil who at
his word departed from the lunatic boy who was "sore
vexed, ofttimes falling into the fire and oft into the
water."[4]

Have you ever wondered, as the disciples did, why
they could not cast the demon out of the boy? Have you
ever wondered why words of healing and of love spoken
by the Master do not have the same effect in the planes
of Mater when spoken through you as they did when he
spoke them? The answer is to be found in precisely this
formula which I have given you on (1) the balancing of
the threefold flame in the heart and (2) the merging of
the coordinate chakras (throat and solar plexus; third
eye and seat of the soul; crown and base) and their
energies "as above, so below." Thus in order to be
healers of mankind and to walk in the footsteps of him
who commanded the wind and the wave, you must
begin by learning the control—the *God-control*—of
energy flow both in the solar plexus and in the spoken
Word.

If you would learn the mastery of the solar plexus,
then I must remand you to the consciousness of the
Elohim Peace and Aloha and their exercise of the
visualization of the great sun disc over the solar plexus,
calling in the name of Jesus the Christ and in the name
of your own Christ Self to the Elohim of the Sixth Ray
for the balancing action of their consciousness to be
anchored in your solar plexus chakra. Visualize a circle or disc of white light the size of a dinner plate
superimposed over your form at the navel. See this as a
brilliant shield of armor like the white disc of the sun
that appears in the sky. Then give the Invocation to
the Great Sun Disc.[5] You may also give the "Count-to-
Nine" Decree [6] written by the Ascended Master Cuzco
specifically for the mastery of the solar plexus, the
throat, and the third eye chakras.

Always remember, blessed chelas of the sacred fire, that our instruction—and above all your application of that instruction—is given in order that you might prepare yourself for the initiations of the cross—the transfiguration, the crucifixion, the resurrection, and the ascension. That you might be prepared for the coming of the Lord unto the tabernacle of being is our prayer. And thus when you have shown yourself "approved unto God, a workman rightly dividing the word of truth,"[7] the hour will come that is appointed by God for you to be taken up "into an high mountain,"[8] into the plane of the I AM Presence apart from the world; and, in the ritual of the transfiguration, your face will "shine as the sun" and your raiment will be "white as the light."[9]

So your countenance will reflect the image and likeness of God; and your aura, as the raiment of your soul, will be filled with the white light of your own Christ Self-awareness. You will find yourself standing face to face with the ascended masters and talking with them as though with friends of old. And if perchance there are disciples of lesser attainment standing by, they may propose the building of tabernacles[10] to commemorate the event and the spot of the converging of the energies of heaven and earth—one for you and one for each of the masters who appear conversing with you. But you will tell them that the transfiguration is not for the exaltation of the personality, nor does the individuality of the soul equate with the human personality or the idolatrous generation; for the transfiguration is the glorying of the Lord in the soul, in the Christ Self, and in the tabernacle foursquare that has become the dwelling place of the Most High God.

The bright cloud that will overshadow you in that hour will be the cloud of the I AM Presence, the forcefield of pulsating white light into which you will one day enter through the ascension spiral. And in that bright cloud is the witness of the heavenly hosts overshadowing those who in time and space are willing to commemorate the God flame—those who are not afraid to draw forth the flame of Spirit that must be ensconced in Matter if that Matter is to be translated in the ritual of the transfiguration to the plane of its origin in Spirit. And so to all who behold the consecration of your life as the transfiguring life of the Christ, the voice out of the cloud will speak, saying, "This is my beloved Son, in whom I AM well pleased; hear ye him." [11]

If you will in earnest seek the mastery of those energies in motion anchored in the solar plexus as a reservoir of light for the release of the power of the spoken Word, the Almighty will sponsor your delivery of the Word of God in this age. And you will be the peace-commanding Presence. And mankind will desire to hear the words that you speak; for they indeed have the authority of your sponsor from on high—the very same I AM THAT I AM who sponsored Moses, saying, "Now therefore go, and I will be with thy mouth and teach thee what thou shalt say." [12] So the same Lord will speak the word through you and will draw all mankind with the seeing of the eye and with the hearing of the ear and with the command "Hear ye him!"

I AM keeping the flame for those who diligently pursue the ritual of the transfiguration.

Djwal Kul

X

The Mastery of the Seven in the Seven and the Test of the Ten

To Those Who Would Multiply the Talents
          of the Lord by the Light within the Chakras:
    Concentric rings of the color rays emanating
from the seven chakras denote the macrocosmic-
microcosmic interchange of energy within the being of
the new-age man and woman. And the outflow and
inflow of energy which accompanies the process marks
the integration of the soul with the causal body as it
enters into communion with the I AM Presence.

    We have described the rings of light which in
the Christed ones are continually emanating from
the heart chakra. Let us also consider that there
is intended to be a continual release of concentric
rings of light not only from the heart, but from
all of the chakras. This release becomes possible
as the individual consciously employs the chakras as
distributing centers for the energies of the I AM
Presence that circulate from the heart throughout the
four lower bodies. Day by day as the aspirant gains
control of the flow of life through his being, the inflow
and the outflow of the life forces in the chakras
increase until the hour of the transfiguration, when all

of the seven chakras, together with the secondary heart chamber, are simultaneously releasing the color rings of the seven rays and the eighth ray from the base of the spine to the crown.

In other words, although the entire aura is encircled by the rings that emanate from the heart, within that aura there are released concentric rings of the color rays from each of the other chakras. And these are according to the petals and their corresponding color frequencies that are designated for each of the chakras, which are as follows: base of the spine: petals, 4, color frequency, white; seat of the soul: petals, 6, color frequency, violet; solar plexus: petals, 10, color frequency, purple flecked with gold; heart: petals, 12, color frequency, pink; secondary heart chamber: petals, 8, color frequency, golden pink; throat: petals, 16, color frequency, blue; third eye: petals, 96, color frequency, green; crown: petals, 972, color frequency, yellow.

Here we begin to see, then, the vision of the wheels within wheels that was beheld by the prophet Ezekiel.[1] Indeed, the chakras are the wheels of the law of a man's being whereby the energies of God are released to and from his being for the integration of his solar awareness in the planes of God's own Self-awareness.

Peter was the disciple who came to Jesus to learn the God-control of the flow of energy. In order to accomplish this, it was required of him that he master fear and doubt and the questioning and curiosity of the carnal mind—all of which issue from the ego's sense of separation from God. Ultimately when Jesus' final test came—the overcoming of the last enemy[2] and the entire momentum of the records of the soul's involvement in mortality—he betrayed his Lord. Jesus' triumph over death by the resurrection flame was his testimony of the law realized in the Logos for the

Piscean dispensation. Those who would follow Jesus must always come face to face with these challengers — fear and doubt, death and mortality — of the flame of Christ-mastery that is the mark of the Piscean conqueror.

One day Peter asked Jesus, "Lord, how oft shall my brother sin against me, and I forgive him? till seven times?" [3] Jesus' answer illustrates the law of the multiplication of energy by the power of ten. The Master said, "I say not unto thee, Until seven times: but, Until seventy times seven." [4]

To forgive is to free, and to free one's brother or one's sister is a gift that lies within your hand. Know you not that when you forgive one another and thereby free one another from bondage to the self, it is in reality you yourself who is freed? Freed from being tied through the law of karma to the one who has offended or wronged you in any way. To forgive, one must be free of fear, of conceit and deceit, of rebellion against the law, of envy and jealousy, and especially of the retaliatory tendencies that beset the ego consciousness. To forgive and to free all parts of life, one must be free of self-pity and the agony of remorse, of ingratitude and that loathsome sense of self-righteousness. But above all, one must be free of self-love, self-condemnation, and self-hatred.

The energies of freedom are anchored in the seat-of-the-soul chakra located approximately midpoint between the navel and the base of the spine. This is the place where the action of the seventh ray of transmutation can be magnetized. And through this ray the misdemeanors of the soul enacted through a misuse of the energies of all of the chakras can be transmuted, their molds (thought matrices) melted down, and the energies used again for the building of more noble forms and for the filling of those forms with noble ideas and their corollary actions.

To forgive seven times is to forgive by the flame of the Christ the wrongs and injustices practiced by the self upon the self and other selves through its perversion of the seven planes of God's consciousness in the seven chakras. Jesus instructed Peter that this was not enough. It was not enough for the integration of the soul into the wholeness of the Christ. The Master taught his disciple that there is a need for the multiplication of the flame of forgiveness by the power of the ten as well as by the power of the seven.

Seven times seven—the period of the Buddha's enlightenment under the bo tree—is for the mastery of the seven planes of being and the mastery of these planes in the seven bodies of man—the four lower bodies and the three higher bodies (the Christ Self, the I AM Presence, and the causal body). Not just one round of seven for the anchoring of spirals of God's awareness in the wheels of the law, but the action of the seven rays in the consciousness of the Elohim multiplying the power of each of the seven chakras. And so for forty-nine days the Buddha sat under the bo tree to reach the attainment of the Enlightened One.

Now hear this: It is the requirement of the initiation of the Buddhic consciousness that you fulfill the law of the seven chakras in each of the planes of God's consciousness. Therefore, once you have gained the mastery of the heart, that mastery must be transferred to each of the other chakras. This, then, will be the fulfillment of the seven rays as the mastery of the heart is transferred to the others. Likewise, once you have mastered the power of the spoken Word in the throat chakra, the energies garnered as the Logos, as the blue fire of God-perfection, direction, and protection, must be upheld in the other six chakras. And the same holds true as you master each of the others.

Having gained the mastery of the seven in the seven, you are ready for the multiplication by the power of the ten. And now we will see why the number ten was so often a part of the ritual and the teaching of Jesus—the ten talents, the ten virgins, the ten lepers, the woman with the ten pieces of silver, and even the dragon having seven heads and ten horns and seven crowns upon his heads. [5]

The solar-plexus chakra has ten petals—five with the positive charge focusing the thrust of Alpha in the secret rays and five with a negative charge focusing the return current of Omega in the secret rays. Thus to the evolving soul consciousness, the solar plexus is the vehicle whereby the initiation of the test of the ten is passed. This is the test of selflessness which always involves the test of the emotions and of the God-control of those emotions through the Divine Ego which can come into prominence in the soul only as the result of the surrender of the human ego.

The desire body, as we have said, is anchored in and releases its energy through the solar plexus and the throat chakra. The desire body of mankind contains a greater amount of God's energy than any of the other three lower bodies. Whatever motives and motivational patterns are contained within the desire body, these are fulfilled both consciously and unconsciously as energy spirals are pressed into manifestation through the solar plexus and the throat chakra.

Mankind are hindered in their fulfillment of the divine plan only insofar as their desires do not reflect the desiring of God to be everywhere the fullness of life and truth and love. When, therefore, mankind, with the determination and the surrender of a Christ in the Garden of Gethsemane, surrender all lesser desires to the greater desire of the Universal Self, then the entire weight of the momentum of energy in the desire body propels the fulfillment of the will of God and the soul's own blueprint is outpictured in the four lower bodies. It is, then, in the hour of the surrender "Nevertheless, not my will but thine be done" [6] that the full momentum of the ten petals in the solar plexus is brought to bear upon the being of man as the multiplying factor of the mastery and the attainment of the other chakras.

The reservoir of light held in the great sun disc, the magnet of the sun presence within the solar plexus, is the energy that multiplies the mastery of love in the heart, of wisdom in the crown, of purity, action, and flow in the base, of freedom in the soul, of vision in the third eye, of service in the solar plexus, and of the sacred Word in the throat. The energies that can be drawn from the desire body of God, anchored in the solar plexus, and released for the blessing of mankind are indeed unlimited. And whether they are used for healing, for science, for abundance, or for the furthering of the arts and the culture of the Mother, they will lend the momentum of the power of the ten and of the ten-times-ten to the mastery of the other six chakras.

The twelve virtues of the heart can be multiplied individually, one by one, or as the wholeness of the balance of the threefold flame. This multiplication, whether it be of the fires of forgiveness or of the five talents, or for the healing of the lepers, is always accomplished through service to life as the true disciple ministers unto the needs of the Christ in all. The more one recognizes the need of humanity and desires to help carry the burden of that need, the greater the energy he is able to draw from the great reservoir of life that can be pulled through the heart from the causal body and then anchored in the solar plexus, the reservoir in Mater of the energies of peace.

Realize, too, O chelas who would expand the domain of the aura by the concentric rings of the chakras, that the energies of the solar plexus may be perverted and then employed to multiply the perversions of the other chakras. And so the seven heads of the dragon, the beast of the carnal mind, symbolize the perversions of the seven aspects of God's consciousness through the lower mental body; the seven crowns upon those heads show the misuse of the seven rays to amplify the seven perversions; and the ten horns are used to multiply the seven-times-seven by the energies of the human will in the solar plexus. Thus, knowing the law, mankind must choose how they will use God's energy and after what manner they will release the energies of the seven chakras.

Remember then the parable of the man who traveled into a far country and called his servants and delivered unto them his goods.[7] The one to whom he gave the five talents is the one who required the initiation of the test of the ten in the solar plexus. The master gave to his servant the five talents as the thrust of the energy of Alpha. In the solar-plexus chakra, these talents are like five positive electrodes of the five secret rays, and they represent the thrust of the Alpha current.

It is up to the soul as it abides in time and space, far from the presence of the lord (the Christ Self and the I AM Presence), to use these electrodes as the masculine polarity of Spirit whereby to draw unto itself through the magnetism of the Spirit the corresponding energies of Omega (the five negative electrodes of the five secret rays), the returning current of the Mother flame that rises from the base-of-the-spine chakra. The tarrying in time and space until the lord returns is an opportunity to prove one's stewardship—one's ability to hold fast to that which is received and to use it to multiply the essence of Spirit in the planes of Mater.

And so when the lord returned to the servant, he found that the one who had received five talents came to him and brought him other five talents, saying, "Lord, thou deliveredst unto me five talents: behold, I have gained beside them five talents more." Thus, having completed the mastery of the test of the ten, the servant received the commendation of the lord, "Well done, thou good and faithful servant; thou hast been faithful over a few things, I will make thee ruler over many things: enter thou into the joy of thy lord." The joy of the lord is the joyous energy of the sixth ray anchored in the solar plexus for the multiplication of the energies of life. Note that only five of the ten virgins passed the test of being prepared for the entering-in to the chamber of the heart with the Chohan of the Sixth Ray, the Master of the Piscean cycle.

This is the hour of the mastery of the feminine ray through the initiation that is called the test of the ten; and the test of the ten is the test of selflessness whereby you salute the Mother ray with the Hail Mary and thereby confirm the balance of the ten petals of the solar plexus, giving ten Hail Marys in each of the five sections of your morning rosary. And the test of the ten multiplied by the action of the five secret rays that form the star of man's being is for the drawing-in through the chakras of the energies of the Mother and of the Holy Spirit. This is the age of opportunity for balance in the heart, balance in the inflow and the outflow of the sacred breath, and balance in the tests of the seven-times-seven multiplied by the power of the ten.

So fulfill the cycles of energy flow within the forcefield of being and watch how the aura will grow and grow and grow. I am focusing the geometry of the aura of the Cosmic Christ until you, by the law of balance, harmony, and congruency, are able to assume that aura.

Djwal Kul

XI

The Mastery of the Flame of Freedom
in the Aquarian Cycle

To Those Who Would Expand the Aura
   through the Freedom of the Soul:
  My beloved, hear now the story of the bondage of the souls of the Israelites — how they were freed by God from the Egyptian bondage and how they entered again into the bondage of the flesh pots of Egypt.[1] Mankind have often wondered why the angel of the Lord or the Lord God himself did not come down from the mountain of the gods to set free the captives of the oppressors, but instead allowed the self-made law of idolatry to render that captivity captive of the law of karma.

  Mankind cry out for salvation, and in the groanings of their souls they appeal to the Almighty. And yet the Almighty has appeared time and time again through his emissaries — angels, prophets, and messengers — to warn of the impending doom that hangs like the sword of Damocles over the idolatrous generation. Likewise, the hand of mercy, of justice, of prophecy, and of wisdom has appeared; and yet mankind, in the perverseness of the wicked, have defied the counsels and the counselors of the God of Israel.

To those who would know the freedom of the soul, I say, listen well! For there is a price that must be paid for that freedom. It is the surrender of your idols, of your idolatry, and of your submission to the idolatrous generation.

And so it came to pass in the days of the judges that an angel of the Lord came up from Gilgal to Bochim and said to the children of Israel: "I made you to go up out of Egypt and have brought you unto the land which I sware unto your fathers; and I said, I will never break my covenant with you. And ye shall make no league with the inhabitants of this land; ye shall throw down their altars: but ye have not obeyed my voice: why have ye done this? Wherefore I also said, I will not drive them out from before you; but they shall be as thorns in your sides, and their gods shall be a snare unto you. And it came to pass, when the angel of the Lord spake these words unto all the children of Israel, that the people lifted up their voice and wept." [2]

Through the hand of Moses, the Israelites were rescued from the bondage of Egypt, which represents the bondage of the soul to the cult of death and the cult of the serpent that arises out of the misuse of the sacred fire in the base-of-the-spine chakra. This is that bondage which results from the utter perversion of the Mother flame. In order for the energies of the Israelites to rise to the plane of God-awareness in the seat-of-the-soul chakra, it was necessary that they be delivered from those who enslaved their consciousness and their energies to spirals of disintegration and death. But in order for them to retain that freedom, to receive the blessings of the Lord, and to be participants in the covenant of their Maker, it was required of them that they should not, in the words of Paul, be "unequally yoked together with unbelievers." [3]

Therefore, God warned the Israelites to be free from entanglements with those who were carnally minded; for by cosmic law the children of righteousness ought not to have fellowship — especially intermarriage and the bearing of offspring — with the children of unrighteousness. For the true Israelites are the children of reality whom God would one day use as the seed of Abraham to bring forth the Christ consciousness and that great nation which would be the fulfillment of the City Foursquare.[4]

But they would not; and their leaders did not drive out the inhabitants of the land which God had given them, nor did they throw down their altars and challenge their gods. And generations arose who knew not the Lord nor the works which he had done for Israel; and they did evil in the sight of God, forsaking the Lord and serving the false gods of Baal and Ashtaroth. And even when the Lord raised up judges among them to deliver them out of the hand of the spoilers, yet in their perverseness they would not hearken unto the judges, but "went a whoring after other gods and bowed themselves unto them."[5]

And so their corruption was great, and the anger of the Lord was hot against the Israelites who departed not from their stubborn ways. And the Lord left the nations of the laggard generation without driving them out in order to prove Israel and to be the testing of her soul. These were the Philistines, the Canaanites, the Sidonians, and the Hivites. Moreover, those who had been chosen of the Lord to carry the torch of freedom "dwelt among the Canaanites, Hittites, and Amorites, and Perizzites, and Hivites, and Jebusites: and they took their daughters to be their wives and gave their daughters to their sons and served their gods. And the children of Israel did evil in the sight of the Lord and forgat the Lord their God and served Baalim and the groves."[6]

"Come now, and let us reason together, saith the Lord: though your sins be as scarlet, they shall be as white as snow; though they be red like crimson, they shall be as wool."[7] In the seat-of-the-soul chakra, there are anchored in man and in woman the powers of procreation—the seed of Alpha in man, the egg of Omega in woman. And the seed and the egg contain the mandala of the Christ consciousness that is passed on from generation to generation through those who espouse the disciplines of the law and keep the commandments of their God.

The soul that is free is the soul that retains the image of the Christ and is the progenitor of that image in the raising-up of the sons and daughters of God who take dominion not only over the earth, but over the idolatrous generations who inhabit the earth. These are of the Christ consciousness which works the works of God and bears the fruit thereof. These are they who multiply the God consciousness "as above, so below" by preserving in honor the freedom of the soul.

Some among the original Hebrews, chosen of God and to whom God gave the Promised Land, compromised their attainment in the seat-of-the-soul chakra by allowing the seed (the Christic light) of Abraham to be commingled with the Canaanites. By so doing they not only forfeited their right to be called the chosen people, but they also forfeited their vision of God in manifestation—the faculty of the third-eye chakra—which would have enabled them to recognize the Christed one who came in fulfillment of the prophecy of Isaiah.

So great was the abomination of those who had been chosen to bear the Word of the law that the Lord God allowed them to be taken into Assyrian and Babylonian captivity and ultimately to be scattered over the face of the earth. Those among the descendants of the twelve tribes of Israel who remembered their calling to free a planet and her people from idolatry and who had never compromised the law of the prophets and the patriarchs were allowed to embody upon a new continent. They were given another land that was the fulfillment of the promise of God unto Abraham — the land of the I AM race. That race is composed of all peoples and kindreds and tongues who have the worship of the individual Christ and the one God — the God of Abraham, of Isaac, and of Jacob, who declared himself unto Moses as the principle of the I AM THAT I AM and who affirmed, "This is my name for ever, and this is my memorial unto all generations."[8]

Because the original race that was chosen to bear that name compromised the light, the very Christos of the seed of the patriarchs, the opportunity to bear the flame of freedom was widened to include all who would choose to come apart from the idolatrous generation to be a separate people who would raise up in the wilderness of the human consciousness the brazen serpent,[9] which symbolized the raising-up of the energies of the Divine Mother — the serpentine fires of the Goddess Kundalini. This is indeed the caduceus action rising as the life force, the energy that blossomed as Aaron's rod[10] through the union of the spirals of Alpha and Omega.

Thus, beloved — and I speak to all children of the I AM THAT I AM in every nation upon earth — the mastery of the seat-of-the-soul chakra is the mastery of the flame of freedom in the Aquarian cycle. It is the retaining of the energy of the seed and the egg in preparation for the bringing forth of Christed ones of the seventh root race. And it is the release of that energy in the upper chakras in creativity, in genius, in learning and innovation, and in the art, the music, the literature, and the culture of the Divine Mother. And thus the fires of freedom anchored in the soul are not to be used in acts of immorality or for the breaking of the code of the Ten Commandments or for the desecration of the grace of the Christ and the sacred energies of the Holy Spirit.

Therefore, in the true spirit of wholeness (*hol-i-ness*), let the sons and daughters of God who would build the temple and the New Jerusalem [11] raise up the energies of the Mother and of the soul through the resurrection spiral; and let those energies be consecrated on the altar of the heart for the building of the golden age. To you who would have the aura of self-mastery, of soul freedom, I say: Let the energies of your lusts, of your pleasure seeking, of the gratification of the senses be now raised up in the wholeness of Almighty God! And with the courage, the honor, and the conviction of the Christed ones, stand before the altar of the Lord of Israel and declare:

In the name of the Messiah who has come into the holy
    of holies of my being, I consecrate my energies to
    the fulfillment of the spirals of Alpha and Omega
In the name of the Promised One whose promise is
    fulfilled in me this day, let the brazen serpent be
    raised up in the wilderness
In the name of the King of Kings and Lord of Lords,
    let the energies of my soul rise for the fulfillment
    of life
In the true name of the Lord God of Israel, I proclaim
    I AM THAT I AM
    I AM the resurrection and the life of every cell
        and atom of my four lower bodies
        now made manifest
    I AM the victory of the ascension in the light
    I AM the ascending triangle of Mater
        converging in the heart and merging
        with the descending triangle of Spirit
    I AM the six-pointed star of victory
    I AM the light of all that *is real*
In my soul I AM free, for my energies are tethered

to the Holy One of Israel
And in the name of the one true God and in fulfillment
    of his commandment, I withdraw the seed
    and the egg of Alpha
    and Omega
    from the unrighteous and the idolatrous generation
I AM the fulfillment of the law of love
I AM a keeper of the flame
And I AM the guardian light of the covenant of my
    Maker, the Lord God of Israel

The challenge goes forth from the Lords of Karma to those who would keep the flame of Israel in America, in the New Jerusalem, and in every nation upon earth: Put down your idolatry and your idolatrous generation, cast down the altars of Baal and Ashtaroth throughout the land, and reclaim your temples for the Lord God of hosts! And let my people return to the sanctity of the sacred ritual of the exchange of the sacred fire between enlightened man and woman who have come before the altar of God to consecrate their union for the bringing forth of the light-bearers. And let the young who ought to be maturing in the ways of the Christ be freed from the luciferian perversions of life's sacred energies, from the incorrect use of the sacred fire in sex, from premarital exchanges, and from perverted practices that issue from the degenerate spirals of Sodom and Gomorrah.

So let these energies be restored to the place of the holy of holies. For the fiat of the Lord rings forth from Horeb this day: Let my people go![12] Set the captives free! and let the judges render judgment this day! In the name of the living Christ: Be thou made whole!

I am invoking the flaming presence of the I AM THAT I AM around all who have chosen to be the fulfillment of the promise of the Lord to Abraham, "I will make thy seed as the stars of the sky in multitude and as the sand which is by the sea shore innumerable."[13] And I am placing the ring of freedom's fire from my consciousness as a circle of protection around the seat-of-the-soul chakra, the energies thereof, and the Christic pattern of the seed and the egg for the sealing of life within you as the life victorious and triumphant.

Djwal Kul

XII

The Energies of the Soul
Raised to the Level of the Third Eye

You Who Are Free in the Soul:
> The Lord Bids You Enter the All-Seeing Eye!

Sealed in an ovoid of light, the energies of the seat-of-the-soul chakra rise to the level of the third eye for the fulfillment of the promise of the City Foursquare. Now let the ascending triangle of the seventh ray merge with the descending triangle of the fifth ray for the alchemy of the violet flame and the precipitation of the green flame that produce the mastery of the air element in the plane of the mind.

To see is to be, and to be is to see. When you raise up the energies of the soul and of your solar awareness to the plane of the all-seeing eye and when you have the balance of love and wisdom converging at the point of reality, you become an alchemist of the Spirit in the planes of Matter. You who are the handiwork of God, by a little self-discipline, by a little self-sacrifice, can come into the inheritance of the children of Israel and behold in the tabernacle of being the coming of the City Foursquare.

In the all-seeing eye of God the Great Silent Watcher holds the immaculate concept of the inheritance of the sons and daughters of God. And the petals in the third eye are forty-eight for the outward thrust of Alpha and forty-eight for the inward thrust of Omega. In the vision of the Christ is the protection of the hereditary traits carried in the seed and the egg of man and woman; indeed it is in the vision of the Christ that the attributes which the Lord God impressed upon the image and likeness of himself in male and female are held. Each of the petals of the third-eye chakra focuses the guardian action of the law and the blueprint of life that is focused in the chromosomes and genes. Moreover, the forty-eight pairs of petals are for the anchoring of the twelve aspects of God's consciousness in each of the four lower bodies as they represent the four sides of the pyramid of life. [1]

Every soul that would be free must accept the challenge to be the fullness of the law of life and the balance of the threefold flame in manifestation in each of the four lower bodies. And so you see, when the twelve godly attributes have been magnetized in the heart chakra, they can be squared through the vision of the all-seeing eye of God in the third-eye chakra. And when the threefold flame and the twelve virtues are balanced in the four lower bodies, there is the converging of energy spirals in the third eye as the capstone is placed on the pyramid of life in the coming of the Christ consciousness.

The great Master Jesus gave the key to the control of the auric light in his teaching on the all-seeing eye. [2] He said, "The light of the body is the eye"; and he explained to the disciples that the light of the aura is focused in the eye—the inner eye of the soul that perceives life with the spherical vision of the mind of God. While the eyes of mankind observe the passing scenes, the scenarios of life experienced in time and space, the eye of the soul is continually interpolating patterns of causation, angles of perfection, the very building blocks of the creation which underlie all experience in the planes of Mater. Thus while the outer man takes life at its face value, the soul is evaluating the flow of energy, of karma, and of the cycles of life from the standpoint of inner reality.

The training given to the Virgin Mary as she prepared the temple for the coming of the Christed One for a mission in the womb of time and space was in the exercise of the faculty of God-vision through the power of concentration. Concentration is the focusing of the energies of the heart in the third-eye chakra as a concentrated beam of emerald hue which penetrates atomic particles, molecules of being, and cells of consciousness, drawing them into alignment with the original blueprint of the creation.

Constancy is another attribute of the overcomers which Mary learned to apply; for constancy is the ritual of applying the fifth ray to the tasks at hand in order that every deed that is done, every service that is rendered, be fulfilled according to the lines of force, the molecules of identity that govern the manifestations of Christed man and Christed woman. Through concentration, then, as a concentrated flow of light through the forty-eight pairs of petals in the third-eye chakra, mankind may master the planes of Mater in the God-controlled release of energy from the planes of Spirit.

"If therefore thine eye be single, thy whole body shall be full of light." The single-eyed vision of which Jesus spoke is the converging of the six-pointed star of Christed awareness in the third eye. When this is accomplished, man and woman are perpetually aware of reality; and through that awareness, life in the four octaves of selfhood is ever consecrated to the Holy Spirit. And the flow of energy through the grids and forcefields of the twelve godly attributes makes the whole body in the planes of God's consciousness—in fire, air, water, and earth—"full of light."

In order to be perfection, man must see perfection. The goal of those who are on the ascending spiral of being is the perfection of the original Monad, the I AM Presence. To accept perfection not only as the goal of life but as the law of life is to enter the path of initiation—*i-niche-i-action.* Initiation begins when that which affirms *I AM,* that which has an awareness of selfhood, secures itself in the *niche* of the all-seeing *eye* of God for the purpose of establishing right *action* on earth as it is in heaven.

All who would understand the miracle of the expanding circles of awareness manifest in and as the aura must come to the realization that the image and likeness of God, the pattern of the Christ out of which male and female were created,[3] is held in the third eye of each one as the potential which every living soul is destined to fulfill. The majority of mankind fail to make contact with that potential which is the image of the Real Self. Lifetime after lifetime, the image remains latent, the soul is not quickened, the consciousness is unmoved, and mankind go their separatist ways according to their perceptions of duality and the two-eyed vision of the outer consciousness that always perceives life as linear, as relative.

Through the sedimentation of the centuries, layer upon layer of effluvia cover over the glorious vision of the all-seeing eye of God manifest in man. And even when energies flow through the third-eye chakra, because of the energy veil that covers over this orifice of reality, mankind wrongly exercise the faculty of God-seeing. Thus Jesus warned, "But if thine eye be evil, thy whole body shall be full of darkness"; that is, if the third eye be contaminated with the energy veil, then the four lower bodies will be filled with that darkness which manifests as the result of the misqualification, or the misuse, of the energies of the third eye.

And so the Master expounded on the conse-
quences of the evil eye: "If therefore the light that is
in thee be darkness, how great is that darkness!" He
explained to his disciples: If the light which the Lord
thy God giveth thee be qualified as darkness, how great
is the momentum of that darkness to perpetuate
life in terror and in trauma. Finally the Master gave
the formula for living in the wholeness of the City
Foursquare: "No man can serve two masters: for either
he will hate the one and love the other; or else he will
hold to the one and despise the other. Ye cannot serve
God and mammon." His inner teaching to the disciples
was that no one can simultaneously hold the vision of
perfection and imperfection: no one can gaze at once
upon the image of Christ and the image of Satan.

This division of the consciousness between the
way of God and the ways of the world is calculated
ultimately to destroy the soul and its opportunity
for Godward evolution. Therefore you see that the
temptation to eat of the fruit of the tree of the
knowledge of good and evil[4] is the first step in the plot
of the fallen ones, whose *modus operandi* is always
divide and conquer. To divide the body of God upon
earth, to split the consciousness of the individual, to
sunder being — driving wedges between the four lower
bodies and the soul, causing schism within and without, and ultimately the destruction of both the human
and the divine personality through a loss of contact
with the material as well as the spiritual environ-
ments — this is the intent of the fallen ones bent on
the destruction, one by one, of each individual frame-
work of identity.

It is not possible for mankind to serve the carnal
mind and the Christed One simultaneously. Therefore
the challenge is given to the stalwart and the true to
purify the center that has been established for the
anchoring of the vision of God and of the perfect

pattern of being and to let the energies that have been trained to focus on duality be raised to the plane of oneness. As the Psalmist said: "I will lift up mine eyes unto the hills, from whence cometh my help. My help cometh from the Lord [the impersonal-personal law], which made heaven and earth."[5]

Let vision flow from the upper reaches of consciousness! Let vision flow back to God and be tethered to the blueprint out of which all things were made! And know, O disciples of the law, that he that keepeth the house of reality is ever beholding perfection within you, through you, as the consciousness of the all-seeing eye. Indeed, the Lord, the Christed One of yourself, is thy keeper[6]—keeping the way of the Tree of Life, keeping the flow of energy, keeping the flame within the heart. Thus that Christed One within you *is* the all-seeing, all-knowing, all-loving One who preserves thee from all aspects of the energy veil that would becloud the mind and the consciousness. The Christ consciousness *is* the preserver of thy soul.

And thus the Lord shall preserve the going-out of the energies of divine vision from the third-eye chakra—of that constancy which manifests as concentration upon and consecration to the immaculate concept of all life. The Christ Self shall preserve the coming-in into the temple of the soul of the energies of the Mother and the Holy Spirit for the balanced manifestation of the City Foursquare "from this time forth and even for evermore." Therefore, let all flesh, all carnality, and all carnal-mindedness be silent before the Lord; for his energies are raised up out of the holy habitation of the Divine Mother (the base-of-the-spine chakra) and of the soul (the seat-of-the-soul chakra) unto the vision of the all-seeing eye (the third-eye chakra).

O chelas of the sacred fire, behold, as the prophet

Zechariah saw through the all-seeing eye, the vision of Joshua the high priest standing before the angel of the Lord and Satan standing at his right hand to resist him.[7] Thus it is in the arena of action, in the flow of time and space, that the carnal mind, the dragon of self-indulgence, comes forth to challenge the soul as it prepares to merge with the image of the Real Self, the Only Begotten of God.

But the Lord, as the law of being, rebukes the energies misqualified in the self-centeredness of the ego. And although the soul, as Joshua, may be clothed with the filthy garments, representing its former involvement with the world, the Lord speaks the fiat of the cleansing unto the fiery angels who stand before him, saying, "Take away the filthy garments from him"; and unto the soul the declaration of the law of forgiveness in the changing of garments is given: "Behold, I have caused thine iniquity to pass from thee, and I will clothe thee with change of raiment." And so in answer to the command of the Lord, they set a fair mitre upon his head and clothed him with garments as the angel of the Lord stood by.

And now comes the covenant of the Lord of hosts made unto every soul who will slay the dragon of the not-self, the false identity that has claimed the kingdom of the seat-of-the-soul chakra and perverted there the image of the True Self held in the all-seeing eye of God: "If thou wilt walk in my ways and if thou wilt keep my charge, then thou shalt also judge my house and shalt also keep my courts, and I will give thee places to walk among these that stand by. Hear now, O Joshua the high priest, thou and thy fellows that sit before thee: for they are men wondered at: for, behold, I will bring forth my servant the BRANCH."

This is the promise to every soul that will overcome idolatry in the seat of the soul and who will return to one God and one Christ perceived as the law

of immaculate selfhood. "For behold the stone that I
have laid before [the soul of] Joshua; upon one stone
[the rock of Christ] shall be seven eyes." This is the
Lord's promise of the transformation of the soul consciousness into the Christ consciousness through the
raising-up of the energies from the level of the seat-of-
the-soul chakra to the level of the third eye.

Therefore Christ—the Promised One, the Messiah—shall come into thy being, into the citadel of
thy consciousness. And the seven eyes indicate the
mastery of the seven rays of the Christ consciousness in
the seven chakras which comes about through the
mastery of the single-eyed vision of the Lord. "Behold,
I will engrave the graving thereof, saith the Lord of
hosts, and I will remove the iniquity of that land in one
day." And so in one cycle as the fulfillment of the
round of the expression of God's consciousness through
the seven rays shall the transmutation of the sin of the
Israelites be accomplished.

And in that day, when the souls of the true
Israelites accept the covenant of their Maker, then
shall they call every man neighbor in the confraternity
of souls who recognize the flame of life as held in
common by all. In that day shall the members of the
body of God in the house of Israel be found under the
vine of the Christ and under the direction of the
individual Christ Self. And they shall make suppli-
cation unto the Lord of being under the fig tree—
the I AM THAT I AM—the great Presence of the
Monad of Life revealed as the one true God.

Then shall Joshua the high priest—the soul that
has been vindicated in the sacred fires of the Holy
Spirit—be made the true head of the Church as he
takes dominion in the New Jerusalem through the
single-eyed vision of the Christ. And Zerubbabel,
representing the state, the energies of Mater conquered in the soul and converging in the third eye

as the City Foursquare, fulfills the balance of the foundations of the law as the head of the state. Now God-government reigns throughout the world of the individual and the nations because mankind have conquered the enemy within and without "not by might nor by power, but by my Spirit [the I AM Presence], saith the Lord of hosts."[8]

Thus in the mastery of the air element through the seat-of-the-soul chakra and the third eye, heart and head, church and state, Spirit and Matter, are one in the harmony of the six-pointed star. And the two anointed ones stand by the Lord of the whole earth with those seven which are the eyes of the Lord[9]—the seven chakras that are the windows of the soul—while the seven Elohim, the seven Spirits of God, anchor in mankind and in the planetary body the energies of the seven rays "which run [flow] to and fro through the whole earth."[10] The olive trees are the messengers of the Lord who in every age proclaim the balance of Alpha and Omega in church and in state and in the life of God lived triumphantly here and now.

I AM for the balanced manifestation of the light within an expanding auric forcefield destined to be of planetary dimension,

Djwal Kul

XIII

The Raising-Up
of the Energies of the Mother

To Those Who Would Flow
    with the River of Water of Life:
    From the fount of the Mother arise the energies of
the Trinity—of Mother, Son, and Holy Spirit—sacred
Mater-realization of the law, the Logos, and the life.
    In the four petals of the base-of-the-spine chakra
is the opportunity for the mastery of self in Matter, for
taking dominion over earth, air, fire, and water. The
base of the spine is the very foundation of life in form.
It is the square of the base of the pyramid that is built
line upon line by the wise master builders who have
learned to focus the threefold flame of the heart not
only in the center of the pyramid, but also in the center
of every stone that is laid according to the chief
cornerstone, the Christ consciousness without which no
other stone is laid that is laid.
    The four petals of the Mother are for the anchor-
ing in Matter-form of the action of the squaring of
the fires of the heart whereby the circle of infinity
becomes the cube of God Self-awareness in time and
space. The four petals form the base of the figure-eight
pattern—even the flow of the caduceus—that crosses

in the heart of man and reaches its culmination in the crown of life. These four petals symbolize twin flames mastering the energies of life "as above, so below"— plus and minus in Alpha, plus and minus in Omega. Whether in Spirit or in Mater, in the flame of the Divine Mother twin flames converge for the union of the energies of life that are for the emancipation of the Christ consciousness in all. White light bursts forth as a thousand suns signal across the skies the fohatic emanations of the eternal Logos.

> In the base of the spine,
> A geometry of harmony sublime,
> The Mother cradles primal essence
> For the realization here and now
> Of Father, Son, and Holy Spirit's vow.
> In the cradle of the Mother
> Is the Manchild's sphere.
> In the cradle of the Mother
> Are the hieroglyphs of Spirit
> And the lexicon of the law.
> In the cradle of the Mother
> Is a diamond without flaw
> And the crystal-clear water
> Flowing as the river of life.
> In the cradle of the Mother
> Is child-man waiting to be born.
> In the cradle of the Mother
> Is the coming of a golden morn.

When the Holy Ghost came upon the virgin consciousness of Mary as she exemplified the Mother ray [Ma-ray] and the power of the Highest over-shadowed her, there was the converging in her womb of the energies of Alpha and Omega for the fulfill-ment of the promise of the coming of Messias.[1] By her devotion to the Mother ray and to the immacu-late concept of the soul of Christ, Mary had magne-

tized in her four lower bodies and in her chakras an
intense concentration of the polarity of Omega.

The awareness of God as Mother was so real
within the consciousness of Mary and her identification
of self in and as the Mother flame was so complete that
in the true understanding of the self as God, she
became in the plane of Mater God's own awareness of
Self as Mother. Hence the salutation of Gabriel, "Hail,
thou that art highly favoured, *the Lord is with thee:*
blessed art thou among women." [2] Among the generations of the *womb man*ifestation, Mary excelled and
was highly favored with grace—the grace of Spirit,
of Alpha. But this favoring was the fulfillment of the
law; for that portion of the Cosmic Virgin which she
had garnered in Matter was the magnetization factor
whereby the Holy Ghost and the seed of the Most High
God converged in her womb for the immaculate
conception of Jesus, the Christed One.

The Magnificat of Mary recorded in the first
chapter of the Book of Luke[3] is the praise of this
daughter of Israel whose soul (anchored in the seat-of-
the-soul chakra) magnifies the law of the Lord, the
Word of the Lord, and the seed of the Holy Ghost.
And the rejoicing of her spirit is the buoyant energy of
the I AM Presence flowing through her being and
throughout all of her centers—the light of her God and
her Saviour.

In the Magnificat Mary utters forth her praise of
the I AM Presence who has regarded the "low estate of
his handmaiden." This blessed one realized that but
for the Spirit of the I AM THAT I AM, the energies of
the Mother in the base of the spine would remain
quiescent. But with the moving of that Spirit in her
being, she recognized the fountain of life springing
forth—with all generations, all cyclings of energies
from the chakras, affirming the blessedness of the
rising flow of the Mother flame.

Mary, a true daughter of Israel, sanctifies the name of God, I AM THAT I AM, and affirms that name as the power of the conception of the Christ. And thereby she confirms the vision of his great mercy and strength, of his judgments, and of the scattering of the proud who have misused the energies of God in the imaginations of their hearts. She acknowledges the exaltation of the energies of life and the putting-down of the mighty from their seats — from their positions of worldly power gained by the positioning of the ego in the seats of the chakras where Christ ought to be enthroned. In the true Spirit of prophecy, she foretells the time when those who anchor in life and in life's sacred centers the dark energies of the ego and the energy veil with which it surrounds itself will be utterly cast down.

And in those who hunger for the truth and righteousness of the law, she foresees the filling of the aura and of the centers with goodly virtue. But those whose auras and chakras are already filled with the miasma of mechanization are sent empty away — devoid of the Holy Spirit. And so Mary, by her acceptance of the covenant that the I AM Presence had made with Abraham and with the seed of the Christ which he bore, became the instrument of the culmination of the Christ consciousness in the sons and daughters of Israel.

When you give the salutation to the Mother ray in the recitation of the Hail Mary, you are giving praise to the energies of the Mother locked within the flame of the heart and sealed in the base-of-the-spine chakra. In this gentle yet powerful salutation, you are day by day drawing the energies of the white-fire core and the base of the spine — yes, even the serpentine fires of the Goddess Kundalini — up the spinal altar for the nourishment and the wholeness of life in all of its centers.

And so, you see, down through the centuries, the
precious rosary given by the saints as an offering to the
holy Mother has been the means whereby the ascended
masters have introduced into Western culture an
aspect of the science practiced by the yogis of the
Himalayas in the raising of the Kundalini and the
purification of consciousness thereby. The personification of the Mother in Mary in the West and the
adoration of that Mother image by all who acknowledge her Son as the Christed One, is the means,
altogether safe, whereby the soul might experience the
reunion with the Father-Mother God in the tabernacle
of being.

This ritual can be actualized in this very life here
on earth without forcing the chakras and without
disturbing the delicate balance of karmic cycles. On a
parallel with this experience is the transmutation by
the fires of the Holy Spirit of the energy layers of the
electronic belt which is comprised of the records, held
in the subconscious strata of the mind, of individual
causation and the memory of the soul's previous
incarnations since the descent into Matter.

The New-Age Rosary, with scriptural meditations
on the life of Jesus and Mary combined with affirmations and adorations of the Spirit, provides the
seeker after the divine union with a masterful yet
moderate method of communion for the raising-up of
the energies of the Mother through the chakras to that
union in the crown which is the attainment of the God
consciousness, the Buddhic light, in the petals (virtues)
of the thousand-petaled lotus.

To all who are enamored with the Mother flame,
I say: The Lord hath need of thee.[4] For to saturate the
planes of fire, air, water, and earth with the devotion
of the Mother ray—this is the goal of life on earth. To
raise up a culture and a civilization that is saturated
with light, light's dimension, and light's intention to be

the fullness of God as "thy kingdom come on earth as it is in heaven"[5] — this indeed is the true destiny of the soul. The more mankind come to the feet of the Divine Mother with praise and with glory, the more they will magnetize the light of Father and Son for the converging of the fires of the Holy Spirit in all.

The world is often devoid of the Spirit of the Christ Mass and of the true Spirit of the law, because they have forsaken the true image of the Mother and erected in her place the great whore and the lusts of Babylon the Great.[6] These idols continually drain the chakras and the aura of mankind of that light which flows from the I AM Presence, the light of the Christ "which lighteth every man that cometh into the world."[7] What a pity that mankind who are the recipients of that wondrous light of the star of his appearing "consume it," as James said, "upon their lusts."[8]

In order for mankind to expand layer upon layer, sphere within sphere, the light of the aura, the old momentums of the carnal mind must be broken and the energies of the Mother raised step by step, initiation by initiation, up the spinal ladder through each of the chakras until the rippling of life in the ecstasy of communion is experienced in the resurrection of being and the transfiguration from mortality to immortality.

Those who truly acknowledge the Father acknowledge the Son. Those who truly acknowledge the Son acknowledge the Mother. It is the light of the Son, the living joy of the Son manifest in the flame of the heart, that magnetizes the energies of the Mother from the base of the spine to the heart. And therefore, those who have developed a more than ordinary expanse of the Christ consciousness do magnetize the flame of the Mother which, when drawn up through being and consciousness, does ultimately merge with the light of the Father in the crown. When this occurs, the Holy Ghost fills the tabernacle of being with a peculiar witness of the wholeness of God.

The ascending triangle of white fire (the energy of Omega in the base chakra) that converges with the descending triangle of yellow fire (the energy of Alpha in the crown) in the crown and in the heart is the fusion of the energies of the Father-Mother God in the Star of David, the star of every man's victory, and the promise of the Messiah. All who strive for this union and practice the ritual of daily offering their energies upon the altar of the heart will increase the aura to its maximum potential, until the aura itself, focusing the Great Central Sun magnet, draws forth the living, breathing essence of the Holy Spirit, and man and woman walk the earth filled with the Presence of our God.

This is the goal of life for you. To achieve it you must follow the meditations and exercises recommended by the ascended masters, including those given in this series. But above all, you must become love, all love, that you might fulfill the law of your being and thereby transcend the law of time and space. I am fitting you for the goal of the alchemical marriage; and I shall give you an exercise for the marriage of the soul to the Spirit of God in my final release in this series.

I AM and I remain in the center of the star of your being,

Djwal Kul

XIV

The Ritual of the Alchemical Union

To Those Who Have Come to Know the Meaning
       of Life Pulsating in the Egg of Selfhood:
   Thirty-three centuries ago, one Ikhnaton [1] beheld
the sun as the focal point for God's consciousness and
adored the light radiating forth from the great sun
disc. The pharaoh of Egypt described the universe as a
giant egg, a great cell of being in which he conceived
the nucleus as the source of that creative force which
he acknowledged as the life energy of God.
   Long before Jesus came to grace the earth with
the flame of the Christ, Ikhnaton proclaimed himself a
son of God and affirmed the presence of that God
within his heart. Not only was Ikhnaton among the
first of the monotheists to come to the fore in the
history of the Fertile Crescent following the sinking of
Atlantis, but he was also among the first of the joint
heirs with Christ to proclaim himself in the identity of
the Flaming One which he acknowledged as sonship.
   Perceiving God in nature and in every form of
life, Ikhnaton was of the lineage of the ancient priest-
hood of the order of Melchizedek, which included
in its descent Enoch, Elijah, Zarathustra, John the

Baptist, Jesus, and many others. These priests of the
sacred fire were one and all filled with the Holy Spirit
and the fire of the I AM THAT I AM which prepares the way for the coming of the Sun King and
the Sun Queen. Ikhnaton was among the first of the
great prophets of the Middle East to acknowledge that
God was a part of all that he had created, to affirm the
great mystery of the Word incarnate. In truth he
proclaimed the integration of the spirals of Spirit with
the cycles of Mater. Indeed he understood the light as
the flow of energy, of love and truth and law, in and
out of material form and consciousness as the very flow
of God himself, God the Spirit who dwelt in the Sun
behind the sun and in the mystical center of the
Cosmic Egg.

All of these revelations, which went against the
mainstream of current religious thought and practice,
including his development of culture and the arts in
the realism of a living flame—these came to the fore
in Ikhnaton because of the purity of his heart and
mind and soul, the clarity of the crystal stream of
water of life flowing through his chakras, and above
all, through his deep devotion to the Mother flame
whom he honored in his consort, the beautiful Queen
Nefertiti, and in their seven daughters outpicturing
the seven rays of the Christ consciousness in the Mother
flame.

We bow then before the flame of one who was
true to his Real Self, who was indeed living truth, and
who left a mark of truth upon the sands of time. And
we call to your attention that the measure of this man
or of any man who would be the Christ is the measure
of purity and of the flow of purity in being and consciousness. By the flow of purity, the soul can bring
forth the full complement of that which otherwise
remains sealed in the causal body, the spheres within
spheres of pulsating life energy surrounding the Divine

Monad of the Higher Self. The soul that swims in the sunlight of God, content to absorb the energies of the higher sphere, the causal body of life, is the soul that comes forth in Mater with attainment, with mastery, and with the gifts of the Spirit to impart to a world impoverished, darkened, and disjointed.

Ikhnaton knew God by the impulse of the soul, even as his soul, adorned in the veil of innocence, was the bride of his Spirit prepared for the alchemical union, for the merger of the pearl of the lower self with the crystal of the Higher Self. And so the alchemical marriage which the priest (the Christ Self) officiating at the altar of the heart is prepared to perform—that is, the wedding of the soul to Spirit—will take place in the tabernacle of being in the hour of the ascension. But along life's way there is indeed opportunity for the precelebration of the ritual of the return.

Each day as you come before your God and before the Son that is the light of the heart, your soul, with the layers of consciousness that make up the fragile pearl, can don the wedding garment in the communion ritual commemorating the hour of the transfiguration and of the crystallization of energies in Spirit when that soul, veiled in Mater energies, will rise from the plane of being through all of the centers, gathering unto itself, as the fire infolding itself,[2] the net gain of the rounds of rebirth. You see, precious hearts yearning also for soul freedom, the soul is the feminine potential, the negative polarity, of Spirit that went forth from the center of being to increase the awareness, the aura of creativity. And by the very nature of its nonpermanence, the soul must fulfill a certain cycling and recycling of energies as layer upon layer its *id*-entity is formed through experience and experimentation with free will in the dimensions of time and space.

Deep within the conscious knowing, that point

of awareness which is in the nucleus of the pearl, the soul is aware of its tenuousness and of the temporal nature of all aspects of selfhood that is realized in the planes of Mater. And thus the yearning of the soul for freedom — freedom to create, freedom to express, freedom to be the truth — reaches a mounting crescendo, an orchestrated movement wherein all of the energies of life vested in that soul potential move with the primal spiritual urge. For the soul knows that the preservation of its life can occur only in the union of the soul with the Spirit, the I AM Presence.

The quest for God on earth is the quest of the soul in search of that permanent identity that can be realized only in the presence of the living God. Through the alchemical marriage the soul becomes a permanent atom in the body of God. And the laws of decay and death and the disintegration of the soul itself no longer apply; for the soul that was corruptible has put on incorruption,[3] and immortality is the sealing of mortality as the place where evil dwells.

The first step in the alchemical marriage is the rising of the primal essence of Mother life from the base-of-the-spine chakra to the level of the seat of the soul. In this action the soul, as the negative polarity of being, increases its awareness of self to the level of awareness of being as Mother.

> And thus the way back Home is found
> As the soul listens to the call of the Mother —
> To her song and her whistle,
> Her lullaby and her discipline.
> Having descended to the farthest descent
> In the densification of God's energy,
> The soul experiences God as Mother,
> And the twain rise to the center
> Where God's energy in motion
> Is the victory of peace and a flaming sword.

Here in the solar plexus
God's desiring to be creator and creativity
Is found to be the impetus of striving.

And with a mighty heave and a ho
And a laughter and "Here I go,"
Soul in the mantle of the Mother
Reaches the plane of the Christ,
Adoring the flame of God
As threefold wonder anchored in the heart—
Mother and Son and a new dimension of life begun.

Whereas it is written,
"The soul that sinneth, it shall die,"[4]
It is also written,
"The soul that winneth, it shall fly."
Soaring sunward to the fiery core
Of the heart's universal store,
The pearled one is attired
In all-transforming fires.

And the transfiguration is the mark
Of the rising of the soul
Clothed upon with the raiment of the Mother
To the plane of the heart
Where the fire of earth and the fire of heaven meet.
Here the union of the triangles
Of all of the chakras
Is found to be the twenty-four
As each star of victory
Reveals a point of identity
On the cosmic clock of Alpha and Omega.

In the transfiguration
The whirling stars
Of victory, reality, fulfillment, vision, and peace
Release the energy
For the transformation

Of every particle of selfhood,
Every nook and cranny of the four lower bodies;
And life below is imbued with life above.
At last the soul has found
The plane of oneness.
No more to go the round
Of the toilers and the spoilers,
The soul confirms the equality
Of Christ-conformity.

Now the Mother Goddess, Flame of Life,
With threefold essence of the Son,
Escorts the bride, the glowing one,
To the upper planes of Spirit;
And the fire infolding itself
Draws into the pearl and into the sacred whirl
The weavings of the Word
And of every word
That proceedeth out of the mouth of God.

Rising to the vision of the whole of creation,
The procession becomes the ritual of the sphere
Reentering the seed and the molecule of life.
And all at once freedom from all strife!
Mother, Son, and soul
Find the oneness of the whole
In the thousand-petaled lotus of the mind of God.
Our Father, our Father, we are one
In the petaled rays of flaming yod!
AUM — AUM — AUM!

Now the trinity of Holy Family,
Father, Mother, and sacred Son,
Merges with the soul to make it whole:
This is the promise and the goal.
At this very moment, the moment of the homing,
The Holy Spirit sparked in the union of Father-Mother

Attends the temple and the altar,
And a flame rises in the heart
To ignite the whole
With the afflatus of the Oversoul.

I have painted for you with words and the
frequencies of my love the image of the ritual of the
rising of the Mother in the soul and the upward flow
of caduceus spirals. At the conclusion of this sacred
ritual—which you can accomplish by visualization,
invocation, and meditation on the thought forms I
have given—the energies recede to the plane of the
heart where they are anchored. And there in the inner
inn of being, the Virgin Mother rocks the Christ Child,
the soul held in arms, tutored by the Mother during
the tarrying in time and space until the soul becomes
the fullness of the grace of the only begotten Son, the
Christed One of the incarnation.

The ritual of the alchemical union as it is
reenacted on earth takes place in the manner
described. But the ultimate release of the soul from the
mortal coil occurs when the soul as the full complement of God-realized being takes flight and the
jewel in the heart of the lotus is released unto the
everlasting arms of the I AM Presence. And all of the
modes of identity, aspects of selfhood, vehicles for the
soul's expression in the various dimensions of Matter
and of Spirit, converge at the point of spiritual
cognition that we have termed the I AM Presence. And
at the moment when in ceremonial rite the Christ Self
gives the bride of the soul to the bridegroom of the
Spirit, the words are spoken, "They are no more twain,
but One."[5] This is being androgynous, being fulfilled,
being God-willed in the wholeness of the union of twin
flames that converge as the I AM Presence of each of
the souls that have issued forth from the Divine
Monad.

Those who are students of the ascended masters need not practice the traditional forms of yoga to attain the immortal reunion. Nevertheless, they will find in these sciences the presaging of the higher way of fulfillment through the energies of the Holy Spirit invoked as the fires of transmutation and liberation. When your aura becomes filled with the fire of God through daily invocations made in the name of the I AM Presence, fiats of the Word, and decrees of definition, there is a pressure that is brought to bear upon the soul and consciousness whereby its true identity, its individuality, is literally catapulted into the Holy of Holies, the secret place of the Most High God that is the I AM Presence.

Pursue then your decrees with all diligence. And know that when decrees are merged with effective meditation, such as that which has been given in the eightfold exercise of the sacred fire breath and other specifics released from the ascended-master octave, including visualization and affirmation of the immaculate concept, you have within your hand the most effective means of securing permanent selfhood at the close of this embodiment.

And for the daily balancing of karma and the transmutation of decadent energies of the past, for the spiritual irrigation of the chakras with the flowing Word of Life, for the filling of the aura with light, for the expansion and the holding of the expansion of the aura, there is no system, ancient or modern, that can replace the science of the spoken Word revealed by Lord Maitreya, demonstrated by the messengers, and prescribed by the chohans of the rays for their chelas who would make the most rapid advances on the path to self-mastery.

The statement "Thou shalt decree a thing, and it shall be established unto thee"[6] from the Book of Job is corollary to the law "The call compels the answer."

You, then, who are advancing in these studies of the human aura, understand that the purpose of this intermediate series has been to acquaint you with the specifics of the application of the law and the light for the surrender of the lesser self, for the sacrifice of all forms of self-indulgence, and for the affirmation of true being here and now in the very plane of awareness where you find yourself a son or a daughter of God.

Wherever you are, whoever you are, O aspirant on the path, hear my word! Take my hand—but not only my hand. My heart also I extend in love and in that divine friendship which is grounded in the life that is not afraid to lay down itself for the Friend.[7] Consider the calling and the cause which we share. Consider that in the simple act of compelling light to flow and to glow in the aura and in the centers which God has provided as anchoring points for his consciousness evolving in man, you can contribute to the universal scheme, to cosmic purpose. And by the application of the law—whatever the cost, whatever the price in the giving-up of the little self—the Higher Self can be won, and omnipotence, omnipresence, and omniscience can reign in the temple of the heart. And then the cell of life which you are as a microcosmic world can blend with and become the cell of God that is the Macrocosmic Egg. Think on this awhile.

As I take my leave of you,
I quote the ancient bard,
Now the hierarch of the age:
"But if the while I think on thee, dear friend,
All losses are restor'd and sorrows end."[8]
Think then upon a friend
Who walked the earth thirty-three rounds ago—
Ikhnaton, a pharaoh of pharaohs,
A prophet of the future and the ancient past,
The seer of a cosmos vast,

Artist and architect of reality,
God's overman who wielded power
For peace and energy, for enlightenment.

For this friend, as the ascended messenger of the gods, stands ready with the invisible yet visible hosts of the Lord to take your hand, to walk and talk with you, and to bequeath to you innocence of soul, purity of flow, and the integration of the stars of your chakras for the creation of the permanent aura of being, the mansion of God-being, the house of the Lord in which is centered the permanent atom of selfhood—the soul that is truly free.

I walk with him along life's way.
I am also yours to have;
And to you I say,
Won't you come our way?
For our way is his way;
And because he has made it his own,
You, too, can make it your own.

I AM for the victory of life everlasting in the aura of the cosmos,

Djwal Kul

Meditations Recommended by Djwal Kul

The Covenant of the Magi
by El Morya

Father, into thy hands I commend my being. Take me and use me — my efforts, my thoughts, my resources, all that I AM — in thy service to the world of men and to thy noble cosmic purposes, yet unknown to my mind. Teach me to be kind in the way of the law that awakens men and guides them to the shores of reality, to the confluence of the River of Life, to the Edenic source, that I may understand that the leaves of the Tree of Life, given to me each day, are for the healing of the nations; that as I garner them into the treasury of being and offer the fruit of my loving adoration to thee and to thy purposes supreme, I shall indeed hold covenant with thee as my guide, my guardian, my friend.

For thou art the directing connector who shall establish my lifestream with those heavenly contacts, limited only by the flow of the hours, who will assist me to perform in the world of men the most meaningful aspect of my individual life plan as conceived by thee and executed in thy name by the Karmic Board of spiritual overseers who, under thy holy direction, do administer thy laws.

So be it, O eternal Father, and may the covenant of thy beloved Son, the living Christ, the Only Begotten of the light, teach me to be aware that he liveth today within the tri-unity of my being as the Great Mediator between my individualized divine presence and my human self; that he raiseth me into Christ consciousness and thy divine realization in order that as the eternal Son becomes one with the Father, so I may ultimately become one with thee in that dynamic moment when out of union is born my perfect freedom to move, to think, to create, to design, to fulfill, to inhabit, to inherit, to dwell and to be wholly within the fullness of thy light.

Father, into thy hands I commend my being.

Note: This meditation is mentioned by Djwal Kul on pages 15-16.

Introit to the Holy Christ Flame

In the name of the beloved mighty victorious Presence of God, I AM in me, my very own beloved Holy Christ Self, beloved Lanello, the entire Spirit of the Great White Brotherhood and the World Mother, elemental life—fire, air, water, and earth! and through the magnetic power of the sacred fire vested within the threefold flame of love, wisdom, and power burning within my heart, I decree:

1. Holy Christ Self above me,
   Thou balance of my soul,
   Let thy blessed radiance
   Descend and make me whole.

Refrain: Thy flame within me ever blazes,
   Thy peace about me ever raises,
   Thy love protects and holds me,
   Thy dazzling light enfolds me.
   I AM thy threefold radiance,
   I AM thy living presence
   Expanding, expanding, expanding now.

2. Holy Christ flame within me,
   Come, expand thy triune light;
   Flood my being with the essence
   Of the pink, blue, gold, and white.

3. Holy lifeline to my Presence,
   Friend and brother ever dear,
   Let me keep thy holy vigil,
   Be thyself in action here.

And in full faith I consciously accept this manifest, manifest, manifest (3x) right here and now with full power, eternally sustained, all-powerfully active, ever expanding, and world enfolding until all are wholly ascended in the light and free! Beloved I AM, beloved I AM, beloved I AM!

Note: The above meditation, or decree, is mentioned by Djwal Kul on page 19. An explanation of decrees and how they work is given in *The Science of the Spoken Word* by Mark and Elizabeth Prophet published by The Summit Lighthouse. A complete selection of decrees and songs is available in *Prayers, Meditations, and Dynamic Decrees for the Coming Revolution in Higher Consciousness* and *The Summit Lighthouse Book of Songs.*

THE CHART OF YOUR DIVINE SELF

The Chart of Your Divine Self

There are three figures represented in the Chart, which we will refer to as the upper figure, the middle figure, and the lower figure.

The upper figure is the I AM Presence, the I AM THAT I AM, the individualization of God's presence for every son and daughter of the Most High.

The Divine Monad consists of the I AM Presence surrounded by the spheres (color rings) of light which comprise the causal body. This is the body of First Cause that contains within it man's "treasure laid up in heaven"—words and works, thoughts and feelings of virtue, attainment, and light—pure energies of love that have risen from the plane of action in time and space as the result of man's judicious exercise of free will and his harmonious qualification of the stream of life that issues forth from the heart of the Presence and descends to the level of the Christ Self, thence to invigorate and enliven the embodied soul.

The middle figure in the Chart is the Mediator between God and man, called the Holy Christ Self, the Real Self, or the Christ consciousness. It has also been referred to as the Higher Mental Body or one's Higher Consciousness.

This Inner Teacher overshadows the lower self, which consists of the soul evolving through the four planes of Matter using the vehicles of the four lower bodies (the etheric, or memory, body; the mental body; the emotional, or desire, body; and the physical body) to balance karma and fulfill the divine plan.

The three figures of the Chart correspond to the Trinity of Father (the upper figure), Son (the middle figure), and Holy Spirit (the lower figure). The latter is the intended temple of the Holy Spirit, whose sacred fire is indicated in the enfolding violet flame. The lower figure corresponds to you as a disciple on the Path. Your soul is the nonpermanent aspect of being which is made permanent through the ritual of the ascension. The ascension is the process whereby the soul, having balanced her karma and fulfilled her divine plan, merges first with the Christ consciousness and then with the living Presence of the I AM THAT I AM. Once the ascension has taken place, the soul, the nonpermanent aspect of being, becomes the Incorruptible One, a permanent atom in the Body of God. The Chart of Your Divine Self is therefore a diagram of yourself—past, present, and future.

The lower figure represents the son of man or child of the Light evolving beneath his own 'Tree of Life'. This is how you should visualize yourself standing in the violet flame, which you invoke daily in the name of the I AM Presence and your Holy Christ Self in order to purify your four lower bodies in preparation for the ritual of the alchemical marriage—your soul's union with the Beloved, your Holy Christ Self.

The lower figure is surrounded by a tube of light, which is projected from the heart of the I AM Presence in answer to your call. It is a cylinder of white light which sustains a forcefield of protection 24 hours a day, so long as you guard it in harmony. It is also invoked daily with the "Heart, Head, and Hand Decrees" and may be reinforced as needed.

The threefold flame of Life is the divine spark sent from the I AM Presence as the gift of life, consciousness, and free will. It is sealed in the secret chamber of the heart that through the Love, Wisdom and Power of the Godhead anchored there the soul may fulfill her reason for being in the physical plane. Also called the Christ flame and the liberty flame, or fleur-de-lis, it is the spark of a man's Divinity, his potential for Christhood.

The silver (or crystal) cord is the stream of life, or "lifestream," that descends from the heart of the I AM Presence to the Holy Christ Self to nourish and sustain (through the chakras) the soul and its vehicles of expression in time and space. It is over this 'umbilical' cord that the energy of the Presence flows, entering the being of man at the crown and giving impetus for the pulsation of the threefold flame as well as the physical heartbeat. When a round of the soul's incarnation in Matter-form is finished, the I AM Presence withdraws the silver cord, whereupon the threefold flame returns to the level of the Christ, and the soul clothed in the etheric garment gravitates to the highest level of her attainment where she is schooled between embodiments, until her final incarnation when the great law decrees she shall go out no more.

The dove of the Holy Spirit descending from the heart of the Father is shown just above the head of the Christ. When the son of man puts on and becomes the Christ consciousness as Jesus did, he merges with the Holy Christ Self. The Holy Spirit is upon him and the words of the Father, the beloved I AM Presence, are spoken, "This is my beloved Son in whom I AM well pleased" (Matt. 3:17).

A more detailed explanation of the Chart of Your Divine Self is given in *The Lost Teachings of Jesus* and *Climb the Highest Mountain* by Mark L. Prophet and Elizabeth Clare Prophet.

Djwal Kul, Come!

In the name of the beloved mighty victorious Presence of God, I AM in me, my very own beloved Holy Christ Self, Holy Christ Selves of all mankind, beloved Djwal Kul, beloved Lanello, the entire Spirit of the Great White Brotherhood and the World Mother, elemental life—fire, air, water, and earth! I decree:

> Djwal Kul, come!
> In the center of the One,
> Anchor now thy radiant sun,
> Magnet of the threefold flame,
> Expand God's aura in God's name!
>
> Djwal Kul, come!
> Threefold fountain, fill my heart;
> Let thy angel now impart
> The name of God—I AM THAT I AM,
> I AM THAT I AM, I AM THAT I AM,
>   I AM THAT I AM!
>
> Djwal Kul, come!
> Flame of gold, pink, blue, and white,
> Seal thy victory star of light;
> Renew my vows to God's own name;
> Come, O Christ, in me now reign!
>
> Djwal Kul, come!
> Expand the fire of the Sun;
> Alpha 'n Omega, make us one,
> Seal my energies in Christ,
> Raise my energies in light!
>
> Djwal Kul, come!
> Align my consciousness with thee,
> Make us one, O make me free!
> Seal my heart and hand in thine,
> In God's mind I AM divine!

Continued

Djwal Kul, come!
Blaze the action of the Whole,
With light of victory fill my soul;
Return me to the Flaming One,
I AM begotten of the Son!

Coda: I AM God-power, I AM God-love,
      I AM THAT I AM, I AM THAT I AM,
         I AM THAT I AM!

      I AM God-mastery and God-control,
      I AM THAT I AM —
      AUM (chant)
      I AM THAT I AM —
      AUM (chant)

      I AM God-obedience now,
      To thy law I vow,
      I AM THAT I AM, I AM THAT I AM,
         I AM THAT I AM!

      God-wisdom flame I AM,
      God-wisdom flame I AM,
      God-wisdom flame I AM!
      AUM — God-har-mo-ny, (chant)
      AUM — God-har-mo-ny, (chant)
      AUM — God-har-mo-ny! (chant)

      God-gratitude, God-gratitude, God-gratitude!
      I AM God-justice in full view,
      I AM God-justice in full view,
      I AM God-justice in full view!

      God-re-al-i-ty! (chant)
      I AM God-vision, God-victory won,
      I AM God-vision, God-victory won,
      I AM God-vision, God-victory won!

And in full faith...

Note: This meditation is to be used with the instruction given by Djwal Kul in chapter 3.

Balance the Threefold Flame in Me

In the name of the beloved mighty victorious Presence of God, I AM in me, and my very own beloved Holy Christ Self, I call to beloved Helios and Vesta and the threefold flame of love, wisdom, and power in the heart of the Great Central Sun, to beloved Morya El, beloved Lanto, beloved Paul the Venetian, beloved mighty Victory, beloved Goddess of Liberty, the seven mighty Elohim, beloved Lanello, the entire Spirit of the Great White Brotherhood and the World Mother, elemental life—fire, air, water, and earth! to balance, blaze, and expand the threefold flame within my heart until I AM manifesting all of thee and naught of the human remains. Take complete dominion and control over my four lower bodies and raise me and all life by the power of the three-times-three into the glorious resurrection and ascension in the light! In the name of the Father, the Mother, the Son, and the Holy Spirit, I decree:

> Balance the threefold flame in me (3x)
>   Beloved I AM!
> Balance the threefold flame in me (3x)
>   Take thy command!
> Balance the threefold flame in me (3x)
>   Magnify it each hour!
> Balance the threefold flame in me (3x)
>   Love, wisdom, and power!

And in full faith I consciously accept this manifest, manifest, manifest (3x) right here and now with full power, eternally sustained, all-powerfully active, ever expanding, and world enfolding until all are wholly ascended in the light and free! Beloved I AM, beloved I AM, beloved I AM!

Note: Repeat stanza three times, using the verbs "blaze" and "expand" in place of "balance" the second and third times.

Transfiguring Affirmations
of Jesus the Christ

I AM THAT I AM
I AM the open door which no man can shut
I AM the light which lighteth every man
    that cometh into the world
I AM the way
I AM the truth
I AM the life
I AM the resurrection
I AM the ascension in the light
I AM the fulfillment of all my needs and requirements
    of the hour
I AM abundant supply poured out upon all life
I AM perfect sight and hearing
I AM the manifest perfection of being
I AM the illimitable light of God made manifest
    everywhere
I AM the light of the holy of holies
I AM a son of God
I AM the light in the holy mountain of God

Note: This meditation is mentioned by Djwal Kul on page 59.

Call to the Fire Breath
by the Goddess of Purity

I AM, I AM, I AM the fire breath of God
From the heart of beloved Alpha and Omega.
This day I AM the immaculate concept
In expression everywhere I move.
Now I AM full of joy
For now I AM the full expression
Of divine love.

My beloved I AM Presence,
Seal me now
Within the very heart of
The expanding fire breath of God:
Let its purity, wholeness, and love
Manifest everywhere I AM today and forever! (3x)

I accept this done right now with full power. I AM
this done right now with full power. I AM, I AM, I AM
God-life expressing perfection all ways at all times.
This which I call forth for myself I call forth for every
man, woman, and child on this planet.

Note: This meditation is mentioned by Djwal Kul on page 70.

Invocation to the Great Sun Disc

Beloved mighty I AM Presence, beloved Holy Christ Self, and beloved Jesus the Christ: Blaze your dazzling light of a thousand suns in, through, and around my four lower bodies as a mighty guardian action of the light of God that never fails to protect the peaceful outpicturing of God's plan through my every thought, word, and deed.

Place your great sun disc over my solar plexus as a mighty shield of armor that shall instantaneously deflect all discord whatsoever that may ever be directed against me or the light for which I stand.

I call now in the name of my mighty I AM Presence to the Elohim of Peace to release throughout my being and world the necessary action of the mighty flame of cosmic Christ peace that shall sustain in me the Christ consciousness at all times, so that I may never be found engaged in a release of misqualified energy to any part of life, whether it be fear, malice, mild dislike, mistrust, censure, or disdain.

I call to beloved Saint Germain to seize all energy which I have ever released against my brethren and which has caused them any form of discomfort whatsoever; and in the name of my mighty I AM Presence I command that that energy be removed from their worlds — cause, effect, record, and memory — and transmuted by the violet flame into the purity and perfection that is the sacred fire essence of God, that the earth and all elemental life might be cut free forever from human creation and given their eternal victory in the light!

I accept this done right now with full power; I AM this done right now with full power. I AM, I AM, I AM God-life expressing perfection all ways at all times. This which I call forth for myself I call forth for every man, woman, and child on this planet. Beloved I AM, beloved I AM, beloved I AM!

Note: This meditation is mentioned by Djwal Kul on page 80.

Count-to-Nine Decree
by Cuzco

In the name of the beloved mighty victorious Presence of God, I AM in me, my very own beloved Holy Christ Self, beloved Archangel Michael, Prince Oromasis, mighty Astrea, Goddess of Light, beloved Ascended Master Cuzco, beloved Lanello, the entire Spirit of the Great White Brotherhood and the World Mother, elemental life—fire, air, water, and earth! I decree:

Come now by love divine,
Guard thou this soul of mine, *(Visualize the white light filling the ovoid of the aura)*
Make now my world all thine,
God's light around me shine.

I count one,
It is done. *(Visualize a band of white fire around the solar plexus)*
O feeling world, be still.
Two and three,
I AM free,
Peace, it is God's will.

I count four,
I do adore *(Visualize a band of white fire around the neck and throat chakra)*
My Presence all divine.
Five and six,
O God, affix
My gaze on thee sublime.

I count seven,
Come, O heaven, *(Visualize a band of white fire around the head and third eye)*
My energies take hold.
Eight and nine,
Completely thine,
My mental world enfold.

Continued

The white-fire light now encircles me,
All riptides are rejected;
With God's own might around me bright
I AM by love protected.

(Visualize the white light encircling all of the chakras and the four lower bodies)

I accept this done right now with full power. I AM this done right now with full power. I AM, I AM, I AM God-life expressing perfection all ways at all times. This which I call forth for myself I call forth for every man, woman, and child on this planet.

And in full faith I consciously accept this manifest, manifest, manifest (3x) right here and now with full power, eternally sustained, all-powerfully active, ever expanding, and world enfolding until all are wholly ascended in the light and free! Beloved I AM, beloved I AM, beloved I AM!

Note: (This meditation is mentioned by Djwal Kul on page 80.) Visualize a three-inch band of white fire encircling the body in a clockwise direction: three times around abdomen for solar plexus and emotional body, three times around thyroid and throat for physical body, and three times around pituitary gland and head for mental body.

The Magnificat of Mary

My soul doth magnify the Lord,
And my spirit hath rejoiced in God my Saviour.
For He hath regarded the low estate
    of His handmaiden:
For, behold, from henceforth
    all generations shall call me blessed.
For He that is mighty hath done to me great things;
    and holy is His name.
And His mercy is on them that fear Him
    from generation to generation.
He hath shewed strength with His arm;
He hath scattered the proud
    in the imagination of their hearts.
He hath put down the mighty from their seats
    and exalted them of low degree.
He hath filled the hungry with good things;
    and the rich He hath sent empty away.
He hath holpen His servant Israel
    in remembrance of His mercy;
As He spake to our fathers,
    to Abraham, and to his seed for ever.

Note: This meditation is mentioned by Djwal Kul on page 110.

Notes

To Those Who Seek a Living Master

1. Acts 9:5.
2. Exod. 3:14.
3. Acts 10:34.
4. Jer. 31:33.

Chapter I

1. Phil. 2:5.
2. Prov. 4:23.
3. Matt. 2:1-12.
4. See p. 125. The Covenant of the Magi was dictated by Master El Morya for disciples of Christ who wish to render a more than ordinary service to God and hierarchy. It is a prayer and a pledge to the eternal Father.
5. Morya was embodied as Melchior; Djwal Kul was embodied as Caspar; Kuthumi was embodied as Balthazar.
6. Matt. 22:37.
7. Acts 1:9.
8. 1 Cor. 3:11.
9. Matt. 22:39.
10. Exod. 3:14.
11. Mal. 2:1-2.
12. Matt. 10:33.
13. Isa. 40:7.
14. Gen. 3:19.
15. See p. 126. See also Decree 30.02 in *Prayers, Meditations, and Dynamic Decrees for the Coming Revolution in Higher Consciousness,* published by The Summit Lighthouse.

Chapter II

1. 1 Pet. 3:4.
2. Rom. 8:5.
3. Jer. 31:33.
4. Rom. 8:2.
5. Rom. 8:6.
6. Josh. 24:15.
7. Rev. 1:18.
8. Rom. 8:7.
9. Prov. 16:25.
10. Mal. 4:1.
11. Mal. 4:2.
12. Gen. 3:15.
13. Matt. 22:1-14.

Chapter III

1. James 4:8.
2. Isa. 55:8.
3. Phil. 2:5.
4. Rom. 8:17.
5. See *Pearls of Wisdom,* 19 May - 25 August 1974.
6. John 1:9.
7. 1 Cor. 13:12.
8. The Sanskrit names for the seven chakras are as follows: base of the spine, Mūlādhāra; seat of the soul, Svādhishthāna; solar plexus, Manipūra; heart, Anāhata; throat, Vishuddha; third eye, Ājnā; crown, Sahasrāra.

Chapter IV

1. Luke 16:15.
2. Luke 16:9.
3. 1 Cor. 15:47-49.
4. 1 Cor. 3:1-2.
5. Matt. 5:25.
6. James 4:7.
7. Matt. 16:23.
8. Matt. 18:21-22.
9. Matt. 18:6.
10. Luke 16:16.
11. Luke 17:21.
12. Pss. 23:6.
13. Pss. 23:1.
14. Pss. 1:2.
15. Pss. 1:3.
16. 1 John 3:2.
17. Matt. 5:8.

Chapter V

1. The seven rays as they are released on the seven days of the week are as follows: Monday, third ray (pink); Tuesday, first ray (blue); Wednesday, fifth ray (green); Thursday, sixth ray (purple

and gold); Friday, fourth ray (white); Saturday, seventh ray (violet); and Sunday, second ray (yellow). See table "The Seven Rays and the Seven Chakras and the Beings Who Ensoul Them," pp. 564-65 of *Climb the Highest Mountain* by Mark and Elizabeth Prophet, published by Summit University Press.

2. Matt. 25:40.

3. The decree is the most powerful of all applications to the Godhead. It is the command of the son or daughter of God made in the name of the I AM Presence and the Christ for the will of the Almighty to come into manifestation as above, so below. It is the means whereby the kingdom of God becomes a reality here and now through the power of the spoken Word. It may be short or long and usually is marked by a formal preamble and a closing, or acceptance.

4. 1 Pet. 5:8.

Chapter VI

1. John 1:14.
2. Acts 2:3.
3. 2 Pet. 1:19.
4. Acts 2:2.
5. Heb. 12:29.
6. Gen. 4:9.
7. Gen. 14:18.
8. Pss. 136:2.
9. Gen. 1:26.
10. Pss. 37:37.
11. Matt. 12:31-32.
12. Rev. 13:16-17, 20:4.
13. Rev. 21:16.
14. Pss. 2:1.
15. Rev. 12:15-16.
16. Matt. 24:24.
17. Gen. 1:3.
18. Matt. 12:36-37.

19. Rev. 12:10-11.
20. Mark 16:20.
21. Matt. 6:20.
22. Rev. 1:13-16.
23. Rev. 1:17-18.

Chapter VII

1. See p. 130.

2. Mary's Scriptural Rosary for the New Age, dictated by Mother Mary to Elizabeth Clare Prophet, is published in the cassette album A8048 and in the book *My Soul Doth Magnify the Lord! New Age Rosary and New Age Teachings of Mother Mary* revealed to Mark and Elizabeth Prophet, published by Summit University Press. A Child's Rosary to Mother Mary is published in the cassette albums A7864, A7905, A7934, and A8045 and The Fourteenth Rosary: The Mystery of Surrender in cassette album V7538.

3. Matt. 6:23.

4. Pss. 82:6; John 10:34.

Chapter VIII

1. See p. 131. See also Decree 1.01 in *Prayers, Meditations, and Dynamic Decrees for the Coming Revolution in Higher Consciousness,* published by The Summit Lighthouse.

2. Rom. 8:17.

3. See discussion of eye magic on pp. 48-50 of *Climb the Highest Mountain* by Mark and Elizabeth Prophet, published by Summit University Press.

4. Rev. 1:8.

Chapter IX

1. Heb. 12:29.
2. John 3:8.

3. Matt. 24:35.
4. Matt. 17:14-21.
5. See p. 132. See also Decree 0.02 in *Prayers, Meditations, and Dynamic Decrees for the Coming Revolution in Higher Consciousness,* published by The Summit Lighthouse.
6. See p. 133. See also Decree 0.10.
7. 2 Tim. 2:15.
8. Mark 9:2.
9. Matt. 17:2.
10. Matt. 17:4.
11. Matt. 17:5.
12. Exod. 4:12.

Chapter X

1. Ezek. 1:16.
2. 1 Cor. 15:26.
3. Matt. 18:21.
4. Matt. 18:22.
5. Matt. 25:28, 25:1; Luke 17:12, 15:8; Rev. 12:3.
6. Luke 22:42.
7. Matt. 25:14-30.

Chapter XI

1. Exod. 16:3.
2. Judg. 2:1-4.
3. 2 Cor. 6:14.
4. Rev. 21:16.
5. Judg. 2:11, 13, 16-17.
6. Judg. 2:19-22, 3:3, 5-7.
7. Isa. 1:18.
8. Exod. 3:14, 15.
9. Num. 21:8-9.
10. Num. 17:8.
11. Rev. 3:12, 21:2.
12. Exod. 7:16.
13. Gen. 22:17, 26:4; Heb. 11:12.

Chapter XII

1. You will note that there are forty-six chromosomes in man. These contain the genes (the DNA) of his heredity which are intended to convey the Christic patterns of the soul blueprint from generation to generation. The forty-eight pairs of petals in the third-eye chakra are for the anchoring of the flame of life in each of the forty-six chromosomes, and the two that remain unmanifest are the white-fire lodes of Alpha and Omega which are anchored in the etheric body as electrodes for the androgynous consciousness that is aware of the wholeness of the Father-Mother God in Christed man and Christed woman.
2. Matt. 6:22-24.
3. Gen. 1:27.
4. Gen. 2:17.
5. Pss. 121:1-2.
6. Pss. 121:4-8.
7. Zech. 3:1-10.
8. Zech. 4:6.
9. Zech. 4:11-14; Rev. 11:3-4.
10. Zech. 4:10.

Chapter XIII

1. John 4:25-26.
2. Luke 1:28.
3. See p. 135. Luke 1:46-55.
4. Matt. 21:1-5.
5. Matt. 6:10.
6. Rev. 17-18.
7. John 1:9.
8. James 4:3.

Chapter XIV

1. Ikhnaton: I acknowledge the at-one-ness of God.
2. Ezek. 1:4.
3. 1 Cor. 15:53.
4. Ezek. 18:4, 20.
5. Matt. 19:6.
6. Job 22:28.
7. John 15:13.
8. William Shakespeare, Sonnet 30, lines 13-14.

Index of Scripture

Index

SUMMIT UNIVERSITY

I n every age there have been some, the few, who have pursued an understanding of God and of selfhood that transcends the current traditions of doctrine and dogma. Compelled by a faith that knows the freedom To Be, they have sought to expand their awareness of God by probing and proving the infinite expressions of his Law. Through the true science of religion, they have penetrated the mysteries of both Spirit and Matter and come to experience God as the All-in-all.

Having discovered the key to Reality, these sons and daughters of God have gathered disciples who desired to pursue the disciplines of universal Law and the inner teachings of the mystery schools. Thus Jesus chose his apostles, Bodhidharma his monks, and Pythagoras his initiates at Crotona. Gautama Buddha called his disciples to form the *sangha* (community) and King Arthur summoned his knights of the Round Table to the quest for the Holy Grail.

Summit University is Maitreya's Mystery School for men and women of the twentieth century who are searching for the great synthesis—the gnosis of Truth which the teachings of the Ascended Masters afford. These adepts are counted among the few who have overcome in every age to join the immortals as our elder brothers and sisters on the Path.

Gautama Buddha and Lord Maitreya sponsor Summit University with the World Teachers Jesus and Kuthumi, the Lords of the Seven Rays, the Divine Mother, the beloved Archangels and the "numberless numbers" of "saints robed in white" who have graduated from earth's schoolroom and are known collectively as the Great White Brotherhood. To this university of the Spirit they lend their flame, their counsel and the momentum of their attainment, even as they fully give the living Teaching to us who would follow in their footsteps to the Source of that reality which they have become.

Founded in 1971 under the direction of the Messengers Mark L. Prophet and Elizabeth Clare Prophet, Summit University holds three twelve-week retreats each year—fall, winter, and spring quarters—as well as two-week summer and weekend seminars, and five-day quarterly conferences. Each course is based on the development of the threefold flame and the unfoldment of the inner potential of the Christ, the Buddha, and the Mother flame. Through the teachings of the Ascended Masters dictated to the Messengers, students at Summit University pursue the disciplines on the path of the ascension for the soul's ultimate reunion with the Spirit of the living God.

This includes the study of the sacred scriptures of East and West taught by Jesus and Gautama, John the Beloved and other adepts of the Sacred Heart; exercises in the self-mastery of the chakras and the aura under Kuthumi and Djwal Kul; beginning and intermediate studies in alchemy under the Ascended Master Saint Germain; the Cosmic Clock—a new-age astrology for charting the cycles of personal psychology, karma, and initiation diagramed by Mother Mary; the science of the spoken Word combining prayer, meditation, dynamic decrees and visualization—all vital keys to the soul's liberation in the Aquarian age.

In addition to weekend services including lectures and dictations from the Masters delivered through the Messengers (in person or on videotape), a midweek healing service—"Be Thou Made Whole!"—is held in the Chapel of the Holy Grail at which the Messenger or ministers offer invocations for the infirm and the healing of the nations. "Watch with Me" Jesus' Vigil of the Hours is also kept with violet-flame decrees for world transmutation.

Students are taught by professionals in the medical and health fields to put into practice some of the lost arts of healing, including prayer and scientific fasting, realignment through balanced nutrition, macrobiotic cooking and natural alternatives to achieve wholeness on a path whose goal is the return to the Law of the One through the soul's reintegration with the inner blueprint. The psychology of the family, marriage, and meditations for the conception of new-age children are discussed and counseling for service in the world community is available.

Teachings and meditations of the Buddha taught by Lord Gautama, Lord Maitreya, Lanello, and the bodhisattvas of East and West are a highlight of Summit University experience. The violet-flame and bija mantras with those of Buddha and Kuan Yin enhance the raising of the Kundalini under the sponsorship of Saint Germain. Classes in Hatha Yoga convene daily, while spiritual initiations as a transfer of Light from the Ascended Masters through the Messengers are given to each student at healing services and at the conclusion of the quarter.

Summit University is a twelve-week spiral that begins with you as self-awareness and ends with you as God Self-awareness. As you traverse the spiral, light intensifies, darkness is transmuted. Energies are aligned, chakras are cleared, and the soul is poised for the victorious fulfillment of the individual divine plan. And you are experiencing the rebirth day by day as, in the words of the apostle Paul, you "put off the old man" being "renewed in the spirit of your mind" and "put on the new man which after God is created in righteousness and true holiness." (Eph. 4:22-24)

In addition to preparing the student to enter into the Guru/chela relationship with the Ascended Masters and the path of initiation outlined in their retreats, the academic standards of Summit University, with emphasis on the basic skills of both oral and written communication, prepare students to enroll in undergraduate and graduate programs in accredited schools and to pursue careers as constructive members of the international community. A high school diploma (or its equivalent) is required, a working knowledge of the English language, and a willingness to become the disciplined one—the disciple of the Great God Self of all.

Summit University is a college of religion, science and culture, qualifying students of any religious affiliation to deliver the Lost Teachings of Jesus and his prophecy for these troubled times. Advanced levels prepare students for ordination as ministers (ministering servants) in Church Universal and Triumphant. Taking its sponsorship and authority from the Holy Spirit, the saints and God's calling upon the Messengers, Summit University has neither sought nor received regional or national accreditation.

Summit University is a way of life that is an integral part of Camelot—an Aquarian-age community located in the Paradise Valley on the 33,000-acre Royal Teton Ranch in southwest Montana adjacent to Yellowstone Park. Here ancient truths become the joy of everyday living in a circle of fellowship of kindred souls drawn together for the fulfillment of their mission in the Universal Christ through the oneness of the Holy Spirit. The Summit University Service/Study Program offers apprenticeship training in all phases of organic farming and ranching, construction, and related community services as well as publishing—from the spoken to the written Word.

Montessori International is the place prepared at the Royal Teton Ranch for the tutoring of the souls of younger seekers on the Path. A private school for infants through twelfth grade, Montessori International was founded in 1970 by Mark and Elizabeth Prophet. Dedicated to the educational principles set forth by Dr. Maria Montessori, its faculty strives to maintain standards of academic excellence and the true education of the heart for the child's unfoldment of his Inner Self.

For those aspiring to become teachers of children through age seven, Summit University Level II in conjunction with the Pan-American Montessori Society offers, under the capable direction of Dr. Elisabeth Caspari or her personally trained Master Teachers, an in-depth study of the Montessori method and its application at home and in the classroom. This six-month program includes an examination of one's personal psychology, tracing behavioral characteristics from birth through childhood and adolescence to the present, taking into consideration the sequences of karma and reincarnation as well as hereditary and environmental influences in child development. Following their successful completion of this information course, students may apply for acceptance into the one- or two-year internship programs, which upon graduation lead to teacher certification from the Pan-American Montessori Society.

For information on Summit University, Montessori International private school, preschool through twelfth grade, conferences and seminars, or how to contact the center nearest you for group meetings and study materials, including a library of publications and audio- and videocassettes of the teachings of the Ascended Masters, call or write Camelot at the Royal Teton Ranch, Box A, Livingston, MT 59047-1390. Telephone: (406) 222-8300.

Summit University does not discriminate on the basis of race, color, sex, national or ethnic origin in its admission policies, programs, and activities.

FOR MORE INFORMATION

For information about the Keepers of the Flame fraternity and monthly lessons; dictations of the Ascended Masters published weekly as Pearls of Wisdom; Summit University three-month and weekend retreats; two-week summer seminars and quarterly conferences which convene at the Royal Teton Ranch, a 33,000-acre self-sufficient spiritual community-in-the-making, as well as the Summit University Service/Study Program with apprenticeship in all phases of organic farming, ranching, macrobiotic cooking, construction, publishing and related community services; Montessori International private school, preschool through twelfth grade for children of Keepers of the Flame; and the Ascended Masters' library and study center nearest you, call or write Summit University Press, Box A, Livingston, Montana 59047-1390. Telephone: (406) 222-8300.

Paperback books, audio- and videocassettes on the teachings of the Ascended Masters dictated to their Messengers, Mark L. Prophet and Elizabeth Clare Prophet — including a video series of Ascended Master dictations on "Prophecy in the New Age," a Summit University Forum TV series with Mrs. Prophet interviewing outstanding experts in the field of health and Nature's alternatives to healing, and another on the defense of freedom — are available through Summit University Press. Write for free catalogue and information packet.

Upon your request we are also happy to send you particulars on this summer's international conference at the Royal Teton Ranch — survival seminars, wilderness treks, teachings of Saint Germain, dictations from the Ascended Masters, prophecy on political and social issues, initiation through the Messenger of the Great White Brotherhood, meditation, yoga, the science of the spoken Word, children's program, summer camping and RV accommodations, and homesteading at Glastonbury.

All at the ranch send you our hearts' love and a joyful welcome to the Inner Retreat!

SUMMIT UNIVERSITY ❧ PRESS®

BOOKS IN PRINT

SAINT GERMAIN ON ALCHEMY
For the Adept in the Aquarian Age
50-page illustrated section
105-page glossary of new-age terms 544 pp. $5.95

SAINT GERMAIN ON PROPHECY
Coming World Changes
Nostradamus on U.S./U.S.S.R. Confrontation
War in Europe • Earthquakes • Chernobyl
608 pp. $5.95

LORDS OF THE SEVEN RAYS
Mirror of Consciousness
608 pp. $5.95

THE HUMAN AURA
by Kuthumi and Djwal Kul 304 pp. $4.95

UNDERSTANDING YOURSELF
A Study in the Psychology of the Soul
by the Masters of the Far East 182 pp. $3.95

THE LOST YEARS OF JESUS
by Elizabeth Clare Prophet
Documentation of Jesus' 17-year journey
to India and Tibet
17 paintings, 79 photos, map
416 pp. $14.95 paperback, $19.95 hardback

THE LOST TEACHINGS OF JESUS
by Mark L. Prophet and Elizabeth Clare Prophet
Vol. I, 520 pp. $14.95 paperback, $19.95 hardback
Vol. II, 650 pp. $16.95 paperback, $21.95 hardback

CLIMB THE HIGHEST MOUNTAIN
The Path of the Higher Self
by Mark L. Prophet and Elizabeth Clare Prophet
700 pp. $16.95 paperback, $21.95 hardback

CORONA CLASS LESSONS
. . . for those who would teach men the Way
by Jesus and Kuthumi (Saint Francis)
504 pp. $12.95

FORBIDDEN MYSTERIES OF ENOCH
The Untold Story of Men and Angels
by Elizabeth Clare Prophet
Contains all the Enoch texts,
including the Book of Enoch
and the Book of the Secrets of Enoch
516 pp. $12.95

MYSTERIES OF THE HOLY GRAIL
by Archangel Gabriel—
Special color section on legends
of the Grail and Jesus in Britain 504 pp. $12.9

THE CHELA AND THE PATH
Meeting the Challenge of Life
in the Twentieth Century
by El Morya 168 pp. $4.95

DOSSIER ON THE ASCENSION
The Story of the Soul's Acceleration into
Higher Consciousness on the Path of Initiation
by Serapis Bey 232 pp. $5.95

VIALS OF THE SEVEN LAST PLAGUES
The Judgments of Almighty God
Delivered by the Seven Archangels 202 pp. $5.9

THE SCIENCE OF THE SPOKEN WORD
Saint Germain's Violet-Flame Affirmations
for the Aquarian Age
by Mark L. Prophet and Elizabeth Clare Prophet
242 pp. $7.95

MY SOUL DOTH MAGNIFY THE LORD!
Mother Mary's New Age Teachings and Rosary
with a Challenge to Christendom
by Mark L. Prophet and Elizabeth Clare Prophet
396 pp. $7.95

THE SACRED ADVENTURE
The Soul's Quest for the Will of God
A classic by El Morya 152 pp. $7.95 hardback

COSMIC CONSCIOUSNESS
One Man's Search for God
by Mark L. Prophet as recorded by
Elizabeth Clare Prophet
A new dimension of self-awareness
through 14 steps of initiation 346 pp. $9.95

PRAYER AND MEDITATION
by Jesus and Kuthumi (Saint Francis)
How to really contact God through prayer,
meditation, and dynamic decrees
360 pp. $9.95

MORYA
The Darjeeling Master Speaks to His Chelas
On the Quest for the Holy Grail
by El Morya 436 pp. $9.95

THE GREAT WHITE BROTHERHOOD
in the Culture, History, and Religion of America
by Elizabeth Clare Prophet 448 pp. $10.95

Available where fine books are sold or directly from the publisher. Postage for books $4.95 and $5.95, please add $.50 for the first book, $.25 each additional book; for books $7.95 through $15.95, add $1.00 for the first, $.50 each additional; for books $16.95 through $25.00, add $1.50 for the first, $.75 each additional. Make checks payable to and mail to: Summit University Press, Dept. 755, Box A, Livingston, MT 59047-1390. Telephone: (406) 222-8300.